Mable Hoffman's
MINI DEEP-FRY COOKERY

CONTENTS

ANOTHER BEST-SELLING COOKERY VOLUME FROM
H.P. BOOKS

Author: Mable Hoffman; Co-author: Gar Hoffman; Research Assistants: Jan Robertson, Linda Worsham; Publisher: Helen Fisher; Editors: Judi Ellingson, Carlene Tejada; Art Director: Josh Young; Book Design: Don Burton; Book Assembly: Chris Crosson; Typography: Frances Ruiz, Mary Kaye Fisher, Cindy Coatsworth, Chuck Barlean; Food Stylist: Mable Hoffman; Photography: George deGennaro Studios; Editor-in-Chief: Carl Shipman.

Published by H.P. Books, P.O. Box 5367, Tucson, AZ 85703 602/888-2150

ISBN: Softcover, 0-912656-80-8; Hardcover, 0-912656-81-6
H.P. Book Number: Softcover, 80; Hardcover, 81
Library of Congress Catalog Card Number: 77-83277 ©1977 H.P. Books Printed in U.S.A.

Cover photo: Fan-Tail Shrimp, see page 55.

The Art of Mini-Frying

The art of frying foods is one of our oldest cooking methods. When cooking was done over an open fire, or in a kitchen fireplace, it was much easier to fry or boil food than to bake it. Then, as gas and electric ranges became available, frying continued to be popular.

Large electric deep-fryers appeared on the market and were enthusiastically received at the time. They produced beautiful golden-brown food. However, they required large amounts of oil or shortening, took a relatively long time to heat and cool and seemed best-suited to prepare large quantities of food. Many people put their big deep-fryers on the back shelf of the cupboard and used them very seldom.

A generation grew up thinking that French fries and doughnuts always came from the fast-food chains instead of being made at home.

The new electric mini-fryers have changed all that, returning the fun and good flavors of deep-frying to the home kitchen. They enable you to deep-fry with a small amount of oil or shortening. They are so convenient you can keep your mini-fryer on the kitchen counter or in a cupboard and plug it in just about anytime.

At first, I found it difficult to think of these little fryers as anything more than a glorified toy for small items such as hors d'oeuvres. They cook so well that I was inspired to try bigger and better things. I decided to give it the real test with yeast doughnuts. I could hardly believe my eyes when they turned out so puffy and golden brown, and just about the lightest doughnuts I had ever tasted.

This book is filled with recipes that I specifically developed for mini-fryers. This means that most standard recipes were cut down to smaller quantities because of the size of the mini-fryers. Many of these recipes make 2, 3 or 4 servings. If you need larger amounts, you may want to double the recipe.

During months of continuous testing of many brands of mini-fryers, I have been very pleased with their performance. Most heat to temperatures between 375°F and 400°F (190°C and 204°C) which is the proper range for most deep frying.

By now, you've probably guessed that I'm a believer in mini-fryers. I hope some of this enthusiasm will rub off on you as you look through the book and learn the versatility of these mighty mites.

**Mable Hoffman, author
of Mini Deep-Fry Cookery, Crepe
Cookery and Crockery Cookery.**

Managing Your Mini-Fryer

Here are some hints and techniques to make the frying process easier for you, and the fried foods more enjoyable.

Because frying is so fast, it's smart to have the foods and utensils ready before you start. Although most foods fit into a mini-fryer, you should be aware of the actual diameter of your unit and size food it will take. You don't have to make any decisions about the cooking temperatures for each item because most mini-fryers have a built-in thermostat set for a temperature range that suits most foods.

How much oil or shortening is needed for frying?

Each recipe calls for "oil or shortening for frying." It is not possible to give the exact amount because the quantity required varies with the brand of mini-fryer. Many require 2 cups of oil or shortening, while other need 2-1/2 or more cups. Be sure to follow the manufacturer's recommendation for the exact quantity because the most efficient amount for the unit has been pre-determined by

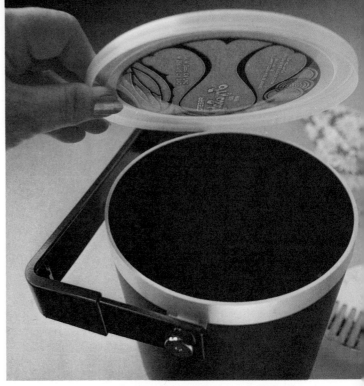

Most mini-fryers have a tight-fitting lid to cover the unit during storage. Be sure to remove this lid before plugging in your fryer; and *never* cover unit while frying. After using wait until the fryer is completely cooled to replace the lid. *Do not store fryer in refrigerator,* even though directions may tell you to do so.

Pour cooking oil, or spoon solid shortening into unheated mini-fryer before you plug it into an electrical outlet. Follow manufacturer's directions for the amount of oil or shortening. Most have a line inside the fryer to indicate correct amount. Do not fill above that line.

Attach electrical cord that came with the unit to the mini-fryer *first*; then plug into an electrical outlet. Most fryers have short cords as a safety precaution.

Preheating time varies with brand, but most mini-fryers take about 10 minutes to reach 375°F to 400°F (191°C to 204°C). A thermometer is not necessary, but if you have a *deep-fry* thermometer, place it in your mini-fryer as soon as you plug it in and you can check to be sure of the temperature.

While the mini-fryer is heating, coat food with the required coating. A piepan or shallow dish is practical for coating vegetables or fish in flour or crumbs. Turn food over with kitchen tongs.

the manufacturer of each mini-fryer. Pour the oil to the line indicated inside the fryer. If you do not use enough oil, food will not cook properly. If you use too much, it may bubble over the top, creating a mess.

What kind of oil or shortening should be used in mini-fryers?

Don't be bewildered when you see the multitude of oils and shortenings at your market. Choose any reliable brand of vegetable shortening or cooking oil except olive oil. For other cooking methods, olive oil is fine, but not for deep-frying. Butter, margarine, and lard are not recommended because they have a fairly low smoking temperature. Cooking oils and vegetable shortenings are ideal because they are colorless, almost odorless, and can be heated to a high temperature without burning. The flavor of the food you're frying is most important, so you don't want to use a strong-flavored oil.

How do you know when to start frying?

The first time you use a mini-fryer, you may wish to check the length of time it takes to heat oil or shortening to frying temperature. After that, you'll know exactly how long to plug in the unit in advance, before you start cooking. Most manufacturers suggest 9 to 10 minutes pre-heating. If you have a *deep-fry* thermometer, put it in your mini-fryer with the oil. Then plug fryer into an electrical outlet. Make sure the thermometer is the type that can be used for deep-frying. Notice the number of minutes it takes to reach 375°F (190°C). Leave the thermometer in the pot during frying, if desired. If you don't have a deep-fry thermometer, drop in a 1-inch cube of white bread when you think the oil is hot enough. If the bread turns a golden color in 60 seconds, the oil is at about 375°F (190°C), or ready for frying.

Once the oil or shortening reaches 375°F (190°C) you can start frying. The temperature will probably go higher than that, and fluctuate when you drop food into it. The thermostatic control built into each mini-fryer cycles the heat on and off to maintain a fairly uniform temperature for frying.

Do all foods fit into mini-fryers?

The recipes in this book are designed specifically for mini-fryers. Because these fryers are made in various shapes and sizes, all foods do not fit all brands and models. Where there may be a size problem, it is mentioned in the recipe, so you will be aware of it.

Why do most of the recipes make only 2, 3 or 4 servings?

In general, the number of servings for each recipe is less than you'll find in most cookbooks because the fryers are small; and they are especially popular with singles, couples, and young families. Also, fried foods are at their best when eaten immediately after cooking, so there's very little interest in frying large quantities of food ahead of time.

What is the best way to put food in the mini-fryer?

It depends on the size and texture of the food. For example, small items such as French fries are easier to immerse in a fryer-basket or metal slotted spoon. Just place a small amount of uncooked potatoes in a fryer-basket or slotted spoon; then lower them into the hot oil or shortening. Larger foods such as chicken parts can be picked up with long-handled tongs and transferred into the mini-fryer. For small fritters, dip out a teaspoon of the batter, then carefully push the batter into hot oil with another teaspoon. If you have iced-tea spoons,

they are especially good for this job because the long handles allow you to reach farther down into the fryer. Doughnuts retain their shape better if you gently slide a pancake turner under each, lift it off the floured board, and carefully drop it into hot oil.

A fork is not recommended for picking up food to be fried. It makes holes, which let out juices from the food and also let more oil into the food, making it greasy.

Why do many of the recipes suggest that you pat food dry?

You've probably heard that oil and water don't mix. This is an important fact in frying. Water dropped into hot oil or shortening will splatter the hot oil. Also, if wet foods are coated with flour or crumbs, they will be soggy instead of crisp or crunchy. Wet foods such as frozen fish that has been thawed, or potatoes soaked in water, or meats that are marinated should be drained, then patted dry with paper towels before they are fried.

Why are different kinds of coatings used?

Coatings serve several purposes. For example, the coating on croquettes holds in the natural

Make sure all food is as dry as possible before frying. If food, such as potatoes, has been soaked in water, drain on paper towels or in colander; then pat dry with more towels.

The metal slotted spoon or fryer basket that comes with most mini-fryers is handy for lowering food into hot oil or shortening. Put in a small amount each time to avoid splattering.

Do not crowd food in the fryer. Give the pieces of food enough space to move around without sticking together. Food will not cook evenly if stuck together.

moisture of the food and keeps it from direct contact with the hot oil while forming a crisp outer covering that's so good to eat. Whatever coating you use, be sure to cover the surface evenly so it will turn a beautiful, crusty golden brown. Some foods, such as doughnuts, do not require a coating. The egg-flour-sugar combination browns easily, creating its own golden-brown covering when fried.

Can the oil or shortening be re-used?

Usually, you can re-use oil or shortening that has been used for frying. After frying, *unplug* your mini-fryer and *cool*. With slotted spoon, skim off any bits of batter or crumbs that are left in the oil. If allowed to remain, they will eventually burn and affect the flavor of your food. To strain out particles that are too small for a slotted spoon, pour oil through a double thickness of cheesecloth. If you're planning to use your mini-fryer soon,

Some fritters, drop doughnuts, and coated vegetables will turn over when they're brown on one side. Use metal slotted spoon to turn over others.

Be sure to drain fried foods carefully as soon as they come out of the fryer. Several layers of paper towels on a cookie sheet or shallow baking pan will do the job.

pour the strained oil back into your mini-fryer; cover and place in a convenient spot in your kitchen, but *not* in your refrigerator.

If you aren't planning to use the mini-fryer for quite a while, oil keeps better in a covered jar or bottle in the refrigerator. Pre-heating time will be longer when you start with chilled oil from the refrigerator.

It's difficult to state an exact number of times that oil can be used. Foods with high sugar content, crumbs that fall into the hot oil, and strong-flavored foods reduce the number of times you can use it. When oil begins to look dark and syrupy, it's time for a change!

How do you keep the first foods warm while you fry the remainder?

Drain freshly fried foods and keep them in a very-low-temperature oven — about 250°F or 120°C—on paper towels in a shallow pan. Add food as it is fried. Remember that all fried foods are at their best when first made so don't keep them any longer than necessary.

Many doughnuts and desserts are sprinkled with powdered sugar. For a fine, sifted effect, place sugar in a strainer; hold above doughnuts and push through with a spoon.

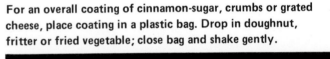

For an overall coating of cinnamon-sugar, crumbs or grated cheese, place coating in a plastic bag. Drop in doughnut, fritter or fried vegetable; close bag and shake gently.

Buyer's Guide

Mini-fryers can turn out a fantastic array of foods. As would be expected, the volume of food that can be fried at any one time is limited but the quality is superb.

Three desirable features are provided by some but not all manufacturers: non-stick coating on *both* inside and outside surfaces, an oil-level mark on the inside surface and an adjustable temperature control. A non-stick coating on inside and outside surfaces aids greatly in cleaning the fryers. An oil-level mark is a visible aid in determining when the oil level has dropped too low during cooking. The adjustable temperature control makes the fryer a multi-purpose appliance that you can use to make soup or stew, or to prepare fondue, or to fry.

Cleaning mini-fryers must be done carefully because most brands should not be immersed in water or other liquid. No matter how careful you are in cooking, oil will splatter on the inside surface, drip on the exterior surface. Because of the high cooking temperature, the oil will bake on those surfaces. The best defense against a build-up of baked-on oil is to select a fryer with a non-stick coating on both interior and exterior surfaces. The second-best defense is to pour out the cooled oil after each use and wash the fryer. When baked-on oil does build up, the manufacturer's cleaning instructions should be followed to thoroughly clean the fryer. In general, for non-stick surfaces, use a good commercial cleaner specifically formulated for these coatings. To clean bare metal surfaces, non-abrasive cleaners and nylon or plastic cleaning pads may be used. I don't know a satisfactory method for removing baked-on oil from painted surfaces.

When you use your mini-fryer be sure to use it on a trivet or other heat-proof surface. Some get quite hot underneath and this could damage some finishes unless you provide protection.

Betty "G" Mini Fryer Model MF55
by Abbot Wire Products, Jamaica, NY 11435
Made of aluminum with plastic handles on sides. Interior surface is brushed aluminum. Exterior surface is polished aluminum. Oil-level mark is provided on interior surface. Cord is detachable.

Wattage: 500	**Oil depth:** 1-1/2''
Preheat time: 15 minutes	**Accessories included:** Plastic cover
Oil/shortening capacity: 2 cups	for storage; slotted metal spoon.
Oil-surface diameter: 5''	

Chilton® Fry Bucket® Deep Fryer Model 88
by Aluminum Specialty Company, Manitowoc, WI 54220
Fryer is made of aluminum with an interior non-stick surface. Exterior surface is painted. Handle is metal and plastic. No oil-level mark is provided. Cord is detachable.

Wattage: 400	**Oil depth:** 7/8''
Preheat time: 20 minutes	**Accessories included:** Aluminum
Oil/shortening capacity: 2 cups	cover, metal tongs.
Oil-surface diameter: 6-7/8''	

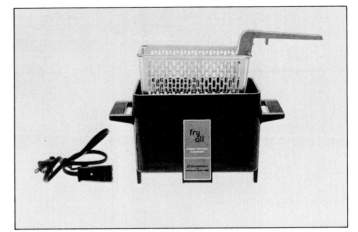

Great American Frying Machine Model 7000
by American Electric Corp., Culver City, CA 90230
Made of aluminum with plastic handle. Interior surface is non-stick. Top 2/3 of exterior surface is non-stick; lower 1/3 is painted. No oil-level mark is provided. Plastic handle warped during first use. Cord is detachable.

Wattage: 650	**Oil depth:** 1-3/4''
Preheat time: 9 minutes	**Accessories included:** Plastic cover for storage; wire basket with folding handle.
Oil/shortening capacity: 2 cups	
Oil-surface diameter: 5-3/4''	

Fry All Deep Fryer Cooker Model 2121
Dominion by Hamilton Beach, Waterbury, CT 06720
Made of cast aluminum. Interior and exterior surfaces have non-stick coating. Oil-level mark is provided on interior surface. Fryer is rectangular in shape with plastic handles on ends. Cord is detachable.

Wattage: 900	**Oil depth:** 1-3/8''
Preheat time: 9 minutes	**Accessories included:** Plastic cover for storage; metal fry basket with folding handle.
Oil/shortening capacity: 2-1/2 cups	
Oil-surface measurements: 6-1/3'' x 4-3/8''	

Farberware® Mini Deep Fryer Model 304
by Farberware®, Bronx, NY 10461

Made of cast aluminum with flared base for stability. Interior surface has non-stick coating. Exterior surface is painted black. Oil-level mark is provided on interior surface. Has metal and plastic cradle-type handle. Cord is detachable.

Wattage: 900	**Oil depth:** 1-1/2''
Preheat time: 12 minutes	**Accessories included:** Plastic cover for storage; slotted metal spoon.
Oil/shortening capacity: 2 cups	
Oil-surface diameter: 5-1/4''	

General Electric Fry Pot™ Model DF 1/3480-212
by General Electric, Bridgeport, CT 06602
Made of cast aluminum. Interior surface is stainless steel. Exterior surface has non-stick coating. Has large plastic handles. Oil-level mark is provided on exterior surface. Cord is detachable.

Wattage: 515	**Oil depth:** 1-1/2''
Preheat time: 10 minutes	**Accessories included:** Plastic cover for storage; wire basket with folding handle.
Oil/shortening capacity: 2 cups	
Oil-surface diameter: 4-3/4''	

The Great Jiffy Fry Model 1702
by K-Mark Corporation, Troy, MI 48084

Made of aluminum. Interior surface does not have a non-stick coating. Exterior surface is painted. No oil-level mark is provided. Handle is plastic-coated metal. Cord is detachable.

Wattage: 650	**Oil-surface diameter:** 5-1/2''
Preheat time: 7 minutes 375°F (191°C)	**Oil depth:** 1''
Oil/shortening capacity: 2 cups	**Accessories included:** Plastic cover for storage; metal fry basket.

Lakewood Jr. Deep Fryer Model 300
by Lakewood Manufacturing Co., Long Beach, CA 90807
Made of cast aluminum. Interior and exterior surfaces have non-stick coating. Has small plastic handles on sides of unit. An oil-level mark is provided on interior surface. Cord is detachable.

Wattage: 900
Preheat time: 9 minutes
Oil/shortening capacity: 2-1/2 cups
Oil-surface diameter: 5-5/8"

Oil depth: 1-1/2"
Accessories included: Plastic cover for storage; metal frying basket with detachable handle; metal spatter shield.

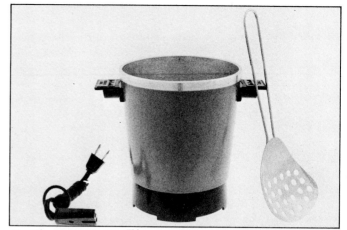

MacDonalds Mighty Mini™ Model 1005
by MacDonald's Home Products, Sparta, MI 49345
Made of cast aluminum. Interior surface is aluminum. Exterior surface is brushed aluminum or porcelain finish. Oil-level marks are provided on interior surface. Has plastic handles on sides. Cord is detachable.

Wattage: 900
Preheat time: 12 minutes
Oil/shortening capacity: 2 cups
Oil-surface diameter: 5-1/2"

Oil depth: 1-1/2"
Accessories included: Plastic cover for storage; slotted metal spoon.

Frying-Hi Model MF 702
by Merit Enterprises Inc., Newark, NJ 07114
Made of cast aluminum. Interior and exterior surfaces have non-stick coating. Oil-level line is provided on interior surface but difficult to see. Handle is aluminum and plastic. Handle of test unit warped during first use. Cord is detachable.

Wattage: 700
Preheat time: 15 minutes
Oil/shortening capacity: 2 cups
Oil-surface diameter: 5-1/2"

Oil depth: 1-1/4"
Accessories included: Plastic cover for storage; slotted metal spoon.

Quick Fry Model MF701
by Merit Enterprises, Inc., Newark, NJ 07114
Made of aluminum with aluminum interior surface and painted decorative exterior surface. Metal handle. Oil-level line is provided on interior surface. Cord is not detachable.

Wattage: 450
Preheat time: 10 minutes
Oil/shortening capacity: 2 cups
Oil-surface diameter: 4"

Oil depth: 2-1/4"
Accessories included: Plastic cover for storage; slotted metal spoon.

Empire™ Little Fry® Model PN60937
by The Metal Ware Corp., Two Rivers, WI 54241
Made of aluminum with plastic handles on sides. Interior surface is metal. Exterior surface is painted black. Oil-level marks are provided on interior surface. Cord is detachable.

Wattage: 600
Preheat time: 8 minutes
Oil/shortening capacity: 2 or 3 cups

Oil-surface diameter: 5-3/4"
Oil depth: 1"
Accessories included: Plastic cover for storage; slotted metal spoon.

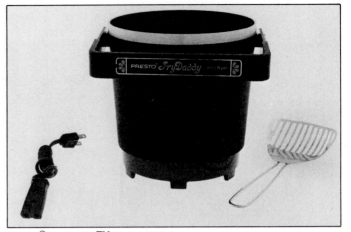

Presto® FryBaby™ Model 01/FBDI
by National Presto Industries, Inc., Eau Claire, WI 54701
Made of cast aluminum. Interior and exterior surfaces have non-stick coating. Handle is plastic. An oil-level mark is provided on the interior surface. Cord is detachable.

Wattage: 900	**Oil depth:** 1-1/4''
Preheat time: 9 minutes	**Accessories included:** Plastic cover for storage; slotted spoon-type spatula.
Oil/shortening capacity: 2 cups	
Oil-surface diameter: 5-1/2''	

Presto® FryDaddy™ Model FDF-1
by National Presto Industries, Inc., Eau Claire, WI 54701
Made of cast aluminum. Interior and exterior surfaces have non-stick coating. Handle is plastic. An oil-level mark is provided on the interior surface. Cord is detachable.

Wattage: 1200	**Oil depth:** 2''
Preheat time: 10 minutes	**Accessories included:** Plastic cover for storage; slotted metal spoon.
Oil/shortening capacity: 4 cups	
Oil-surface diameter: 6-1/2''	

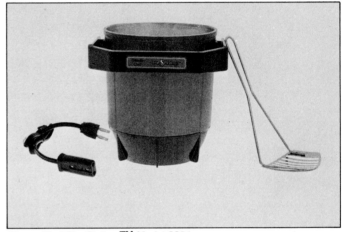

Norelco® Fast Fry™ Model HB 2020
by North American Philips Corp., New York, NY 10017
Made of cast aluminum with plastic handles on sides. Interior and exterior surfaces have non-stick coating. An oil-level mark is provided on the interior surface. Cord is detachable.

Wattage: 900	**Oil depth:** 1-1/4''
Preheat time: 9 minutes	**Accessories included:** Plastic cover for storage; plastic doughnut cutter; metal fry basket.
Oil/shortening capacity: 2-1/2 cups	
Oil-surface diameter: 6''	

Master Chef The Shrimp™ Model 2061
by Northern Electric Co., Chicago, IL 60625
Made of heavy cast aluminum with plastic handle. Interior surface is metal; exterior surface is painted. Oil-level mark provided on interior surface. Cord is detachable.

Wattage: 900	**Oil depth:** 1-1/4''
Preheat time: 10 minutes	**Accessories included:** Plastic cover for storage; slotted metal spoon.
Oil/shortening capacity: 2 cups	
Oil-surface diameter: 5-3/4''	

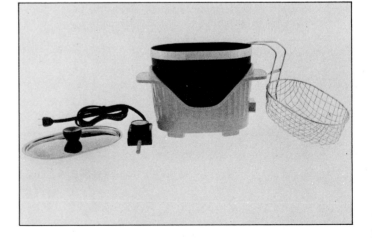

Nordic Ware® Multi-Fry-Cook Model 86000
by Northland Aluminum Products, Inc., Minneapolis, MN 55416
This multi-purpose appliance consists of a cast aluminum pot securely cradled in a plastic holder. Interior and exterior surfaces have non-stick coating. Oil-level mark is provided on interior surface. An adjustable heat control provides a cooking temperature range of 180°F to 400°F (82°C to 204°C). Has oval shape. Cord is detachable.

Wattage: 1100	**Oil depth:** 1-3/8''
Preheat time: 9 minutes	**Accessories included:** Stainless steel cover; metal fry basket.
Oil/shortening capacity: 3 cups	
Oil-surface measurements: 7-1/2'' x 5''	

Oster "Li'l Fritter"™ Model 732-03
by Oster Corporation, Milwaukee, WI 53217
Multi-purpose appliance of heavy cast aluminum; plastic handles on sides. Shape is square. Interior and top of exterior surface have non-stick coating. Adjustable heat control proves cooking temperature range of 170°F to 390°F (77°C to 199°C). Cord is detachable.

Wattage: 1200	**Oil depth:** 2"
Preheat time: 8 minutes	**Accessories included:** Plastic cover for storage; wire basket with folding handle and drain clip.
Oil/shortening capacity: 4 cups	
Oil-surface measurements: 6-1/2" x 6-1/2"	

Flavo-Rite Mini-Fri Model M900
by Reliable Manufacturing Corp., Franklin Park, IL 60131
Made of aluminum. Interior surface has non-stick coating; exterior surface is polished metal. Has plastic handle. Cord is detachable.

Wattage: 900	**Oil depth:** 1-1/8"
Preheat time: 9 minutes	**Accessories included:** Plastic cover for storage; slotted metal spoon.
Oil/shortening capacity: 2 cups	
Oil-surface diameter: 5-3/4"	

Magic-Maid "Petite-Size" Model 820929
by Son-Chief Electric, Winsted, CT 06098
Made of cast aluminum. Interior and exterior surfaces have non-stick coating. Oil-level mark is provided on interior surface. Has metal and plastic handle. Cord is detachable.

Wattage: 700	**Oil depth:** 1-1/2"
Preheat time: 10 minutes	**Accessories included:** Plastic cover for storage; slotted metal spoon.
Oil/shortening capacity: 2 cups	
Oil-surface diameter: 5-1/2"	

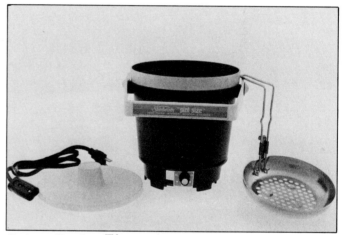

Sunbeam "Pint Size"™ Model 9-69
by Sunbeam Corporation, Chicago IL 60650
This multi-purpose appliance is made of cast aluminum securely cradled in a plastic holder. Interior and exterior surfaces have non-stick coating. Oil-level mark is provided on interior surface. An adjustable heat control provides a cooking temperature range of 180°F to 390°F (82°C to 199°C). Cord is detachable.

Wattage: 1000	**Accessories included:** Plastic cover for steaming, simmering and storage; slotted metal fry basket with folding handle and drain clip. Doughnut holder for fry basket.
Preheat time: 8 minutes	
Oil/shortening capacity: 2 cups	
Oil-surface diameter: 6-1/4"	
Oil depth: 1-1/2"	

West Bend® Fryette™ Catalog No. 5121
by The West Bend Company, West Bend, WI 53095
Made of cast aluminum. Interior and exterior surfaces have non-stick coating. Has plastic handles on sides. Oil-level mark is provided on interior surface. Cord is detachable.

Wattage: 900	**Oil depth:** 1-7/8"
Preheat time: 9 minutes	**Accessories included:** Plastic cover for storage; slotted metal spoon-type spatula.
Oil/shortening capacity: 2 cups	
Oil-surface diameter: 4-5/8"	

Mini-Fry Accessories

All of these utensils are not *essential* accessories for your mini-fryer, but they are items that proved useful while developing recipes for this book. For most recipes, you can get by if you have a measuring cup and spoons, a mixing bowl, a large wooden or plastic spoon for mixing batters and sauces, a slotted metal spoon or pancake turner, and a roll of paper towels for drying and draining.

Although not necessary, I find a deep-fry thermometer most helpful. When I heat oil or shortening, I clip a thermometer on the side of the fryer so I know when the oil is hot enough. There are two basic kinds of deep-fry thermometers. One has a round dial and the other a vertical scale showing the temperature. Some are a combination candy and deep-fat thermometer. It's OK to use this combination. The most important thing to remember is that the words "deep-fry" should be on any thermometer you use in hot oil.

Most mini-fryers have a fryer basket or slotted spoon with them. You can use an ordinary metal slotted spoon from your kitchen, if you prefer. I like to use long metal tongs to lift large pieces of food in and out of the fryer. Plastic tongs are great for coating pieces of fruits, vegetables or meats in flour or crumb mixtures, *but don't use plastic in hot oil.*

A kitchen timer is another helpful accessory. You can use the one built into your range, or a separate unit. When frying, I set the timer to the length of time I think it will take, then rely on it to remind me when to check the food. It really helps prevent overcooking.

Paper towels do double duty in frying. They're essential for patting wet foods dry before frying and perfect to absorb excess oil from foods that have been fried.

Of course, a sharp knife is the cook's best friend for slicing, chopping and peeling; and a cutting board provides the base for these procedures. A large board, or a clean smooth surface, is handy for rolling out doughnuts and small fried breads.

Do's and Don'ts of Mini-Frying

Use mini-fryer on a level, heat-resistant surface.

Pour oil into unheated mini-fryer before plugging it into electrical outlet.

Before each use, add new oil to bring oil to level line.

Use mini-basket or slotted metal spoon to lower uncooked food into mini-fryer, and remove it when done.

If food is wet, pat dry with paper towels before dropping into hot oil or shortening.

Leave space in hot oil so food can move around while frying.

When foods are brown on one side, turn with slotted metal spoon to brown other side.

Occasionally stir food pieces during frying to keep them from sticking together.

Scoop loose particles of food or batter from oil with slotted metal spoon.

Serve fried foods immediately.

Don't place hot mini-fryer on wooden, glass or plastic surface.

Don't use cover on mini-fryer while frying.

Don't use plastic or rubber-coated utensils in hot oil or shortening.

Don't let electric cord dangle over edge of counter.

Don't place wet foods in mini-fryer—they will splatter and not cook properly.

Don't drop food in mini-fryer until oil or shortening is hot.

Don't overcrowd food in mini-fryer.

Don't touch hot surface of mini-fryer.

Don't pick up mini-fryer while oil is hot.

Don't cover mini-fryer until it cools.

Don't use mini-fryer outdoors.

Appetizers

Could you use extra help when getting ready for a party? Let your mini-fryer come to the rescue. It can give you hot crunchy appetizers in minutes.

Do all of your advance preparation early in the day. Combine ingredients for the appetizers you're planning to fry. Then fry them just before guests arrive; drain and serve while still warm and crispy.

Even better, arrange uncooked ingredients on a tray and let guests fry their own appetizers. Everyone will love the idea of having a part in the preparation, and also enjoy choosing favorite appetizers.

Start with suggestions from this book. Then vary the fillings or coatings to create your own recipes. For example, I have included several won ton appetizers because they are so versatile. They are great when you want to have a special appetizer. Won

ton skins or wrappers may be found in Oriental markets and gourmet shops, and in the frozen or deli sections of many supermarkets. They freeze well, so pick up a package the next time you see them in the market; freeze and keep on hand until you need them. They are already cut into squares. Just thaw them the day you want to serve them; mix up your favorite filling; fill and fry. No doubt you have seen several ways to fold won tons. I have included directions for one of the traditional folds, in addition to a very simple triangle.

Be careful not to overcook appetizers. They are small and usually take less time than most main dishes or larger portions of food. When possible, fry a few appetizers at a time, and serve right away.

Fried Cheese Cubes

Melted cheese is the surprise inside these appetizers.

1/4-lb. sharp Cheddar cheese,
  cut in 1-in. cubes
2 eggs, beaten

1/2 cup fine dry, seasoned bread crumbs
Oil or shortening for frying

In shallow dish, dip Cheddar cheese cubes in eggs. In piepan, roll in seasoned bread crumbs. Repeat; the thick coating prevents cheese from leaking through. Fry in hot oil or shortening in mini-fryer until light brown. Remove from mini-fryer quickly. Drain. Cool slightly but serve warm. Makes 25 to 30 appetizers.

Cheese Turnovers

Choose your favorite kind of cheese!

2 cups flour
1 teaspoon salt
1 teaspoon baking powder
1 teaspoon chili powder
1/2 cup milk

1 egg
1/4 cup butter or margarine, melted
Oil or shortening for frying
Cheese Filling, see below

Cheese Filling:
2 tablespoons green onion, thinly sliced
2 tablespoons parsley, chopped
1/2 tablespoon butter or margarine
1/8 teaspoon salt

1/8 teaspoon pepper
1/2 lb. Cheddar or
    Monterey Jack cheese, shredded

In medium bowl, mix flour, 1 teaspoon salt, baking powder and chili powder. In small bowl, beat milk and egg. Stir into flour mixture. Stir in melted butter or margarine; dough will be soft. Turn dough onto lightly floured board. Knead about 4 minutes until smooth. Shape into ball. Place in bowl, cover and chill 30 minutes. Make Cheese Filling. Divide dough in half. On lightly floured board, roll out each half about 1/8-inch thick. Cut into 3-inch circles. Place about 1 teaspoon Cheese Filling in center of each circle. Moisten edges, fold dough over Cheese Filling and press edges with fork to seal securely. Fry in hot oil or shortening in mini-fryer about 1 minute until brown on both sides. Drain. Serve warm. Makes about 14 appetizers.

Cheese Filling:
Cook onion and parsley in 1/2 tablespoon butter or margarine until onion is tender. Remove from heat, stir in salt, pepper and shredded Cheddar or Monterey Jack cheese.

Shortcut Nachos

Fry extra tortilla wedges for use as snacks or with your favorite dips.

4 flour tortillas
Oil or shortening for frying
2 cups grated Monterey Jack or
   Cheddar cheese

1/4 cup chopped canned
   green chili peppers

Cut each tortilla into 8 wedges. Drop 3 or 4 pieces at a time into hot oil or shortening in mini-fryer. Fry until light brown and puffy, about 1/2 minute on each side. Drain. Sprinkle immediately with grated Monterey Jack or Cheddar cheese and chopped peppers. Serve warm. Fry tortillas ahead of time, if desired; then at serving time, sprinkle with cheese and peppers and place in oven broiler until cheese melts. Makes 32 appetizers.

Oriental Appetizer Balls

So good you'll want to double the recipe for a party.

1/4 lb. ground pork sausage
1/4 lb. finely chopped cooked shrimp
1/4 cup finely chopped water chestnuts
1/4 cup finely chopped onion

2 tablespoons soy sauce
1/8 teaspoon sugar
1 egg, slightly beaten
Oil or shortening for frying

In medium bowl, combine ground sausage with shrimp, water chestnuts, onion, soy sauce, sugar and egg. Shape into 1-inch balls. Drop into hot oil or shortening in mini-fryer. Fry until brown. Serve hot. Makes about 30 appetizers.

Fried Cheese Balls

Great cheese flavor!

1 egg, slightly beaten
1/4 teaspoon baking powder
1 tablespoon flour
1/4 lb. grated sharp Cheddar cheese

2 tablespoons chopped ripe olives
1/4 teaspoon seasoned salt
Oil or shortening for frying

Combine egg, baking powder, flour, grated Cheddar cheese, olives and seasoned salt. Drop by teaspoons into hot oil or shortening in mini-fryer. Fry about 1-1/2 to 2 minutes or until golden. Drain. Serve hot. Makes about 15 appetizers.

Clam Puffs

Start your party right with clam appetizers.

1 egg
1/4 cup milk
2/3 cup flour
1/2 teaspoon baking powder
1/4 teaspoon salt
1/8 teaspoon cayenne pepper

1 (6-1/2-oz.) can minced clams,
 well-drained
2 tablespoons minced green onions
1 teaspoon minced parsley
Oil or shortening for frying

In medium bowl, beat egg with milk. Add flour, baking powder, salt and cayenne pepper. Beat until well-blended. Stir in clams, onions and parsley. Drop by teaspoons into hot oil or shortening in mini-fryer. Fry 2 to 2-1/2 minutes. Drain. Serve warm. Makes about 18 to 20 appetizers.

Fiesta Chips

Pie-shaped puffs can be served as dippers or as a bread.

1/2 cup flour
1/3 cup yellow cornmeal
1 teaspoon salt
1/2 teaspoon chili powder

1/3 cup water
Oil or shortening for frying
Avocado or bean dip, if desired

In small bowl, mix flour, cornmeal, salt and chili powder. Add water gradually, stirring until flour mixture is moistened. Turn onto a lightly floured board. Knead until smooth, about 3 minutes. Shape dough into a ball and place in a covered bowl. Chill 30 minutes. Divide dough in half. Roll each half into an 8-inch circle. Cut each circle into 8 triangles. Fry triangles in hot oil or shortening in mini-fryer until golden brown. Drain. Serve warm or cool. Especially good with avocado or bean dip, if desired. Makes 16 appetizers.

French-Fried Mushrooms

Terrific as an appetizer or with roast beef.

1 egg
1/2 cup milk
1/2 teaspoon salt
30 medium mushrooms
1/3 cup flour

1 cup corn flake crumbs
Oil or shortening for frying
Salt to taste
Grated Parmesan cheese
Lemon wedges, if desired

In shallow dish, beat egg with milk and salt. In another dish, roll mushrooms in flour. Dip mushrooms in egg mixture and coat with corn flake crumbs. Fry in hot oil or shortening in mini-fryer 1 to 2 minutes until golden. Drain. Sprinkle with salt to taste and grated Parmesan cheese. Serve with lemon wedges, if desired. Makes 30 appetizers.

Cut chicken wings at joints to make 3 pieces. Discard wing tips.

With sharp knife, push meat to one end of the bone so it resembles a small drumstick.

How to Make Mini Mandarin Drumsticks

Clockwise from top left: French-Fried Mushrooms, Mini Mandarin Drumsticks, South-of-the-Border Won Ton.

After dipping drumstick in batter, drop into hot oil or shortening. If using plastic tongs, be careful to prevent plastic from touching hot oil. Metal utensils are preferred.

Dip fried chicken into sauce; then brush with sauce several times while baking.

South-of-the-Border Won Ton

A tasty change from the traditional won ton filling!

1/2 lb. lean ground beef
1 green onion, finely chopped
1/2 teaspoon salt
1/2 teaspoon chili powder
1/4 teaspoon garlic salt

1/2 cup grated Monterey Jack cheese
2 tablespoons chopped ripe olives
30 to 35 won ton skins or wrappers
Oil or shortening for frying

In small skillet, break up beef with a fork. Cook with onion, salt, chili powder and garlic salt for several minutes. Stir in grated Monterey Jack cheese and olives. Cool slightly. Place about 1 rounded teaspoon filling in center of each won ton skin. Moisten edges of skin. Fold 2 opposite corners together, forming a triangle. Seal edges. Drop into hot oil or shortening in mini-fryer. Fry about 1 minute, until crisp and golden. Drain. Serve hot. Good plain or with guacamole sauce, if desired. Makes 30 to 35 appetizers.

Mini Mandarin Drumsticks

Bake on the spicy glaze just before your guests arrive.

12 chicken wings
1/2 cup cornstarch
1 egg, slightly beaten
1/4 teaspoon salt
1/4 teaspoon seasoned salt

2 tablespoons milk
Oil or shortening for frying
Spicy Glaze, see below
Sesame seeds

Spicy Glaze:
1 cup sugar
1/4 cup water
1/2 cup vinegar

1 teaspoon soy sauce
1 tablespoon catsup
1 tablespoon chopped green onion

Cut chicken wings at joints; discard wing tips. Scrape and push meat to one end of bone so each piece resembles a small drumstick. In medium bowl, combine cornstarch, egg, salt, seasoned salt and milk. Mix until smooth. Dip each drumstick in batter. Drop into hot oil or shortening in mini-fryer. Fry 3 minutes or until lightly browned; drain. Chill or freeze until needed, if desired. Make Spicy Glaze. Dip fried drumsticks in Spicy Glaze. In shallow baking pan, place in single layer. Bake at 350°F (177°C) for 30 minutes, basting several times with Spicy Glaze. Sprinkle with sesame seeds and serve hot. Makes 24 appetizers.

Spicy Glaze:
In small saucepan, combine ingredients. Bring to a boil, stirring until sugar dissolves.

Spiced Walnuts

Bet you can't stop eating these!

1 cup walnut halves
Oil or shortening for frying
1/2 teaspoon salt
1/4 teaspoon cinnamon

1/8 teaspoon nutmeg
1/8 teaspoon cloves
1/8 teaspoon allspice
1/4 cup sugar

Fry 1/4 cup of the nuts at a time in hot oil or shortening in mini-fryer until golden brown. Drain. While warm, drop into a paper bag containing mixture of salt, spices and sugar. Shake bag to coat nuts well. Makes 1 cup.

Fried Nuts

Try a different flavor each time.

1 cup peanuts, pecan halves or
   whole blanched almonds

Oil or shortening for frying
1/2 teaspoon salt or seasoned salt

In fryer basket or small metal strainer, lower nuts, 1/4 cup at a time, into hot oil or shortening in mini-fryer. Fry 1 to 1-1/2 minutes until golden brown. Drain. Sprinkle with salt or seasoned salt. Serve warm or cool. Makes 1 cup.

Variations:
Sprinkle 1 teaspoon chili powder over peanuts.

Sprinkle 2 teaspoons soy sauce over pecans.

Sprinkle 1 teaspoon curry powder over almonds.

How To Fold Won Ton

Place filling in center of won ton skin. Brush edges of won ton skin with water.

Fold 2 opposite corners together, forming a triangle. Press edges to seal.

Pull the right and left corners of folded triangle down and below folded edge so they overlap slightly. Moisten and pinch together.

Fried Won Ton

Try a Chinese tradition.

1/2 lb. uncooked, boneless pork,
   chicken or turkey
2 tablespoons oil
2 tablespoons chopped green onions
4 canned water chestnuts, chopped
1 tablespoon sherry wine

1/4 teaspoon salt
2 teaspoons cornstarch
2 tablespoons soy sauce
25 to 35 won ton skins or wrappers
Oil or shortening for frying

Finely chop uncooked pork, chicken or turkey. In medium skillet, cook meat in 2 tablespoons oil several minutes. Stir in onions, water chestnuts, wine and salt. Dissolve cornstarch in soy sauce. Add to mixture in skillet. Cook, stirring constantly over low heat until thick and translucent. Place 1 rounded teaspoon of filling in center of each won ton skin. Moisten edges of skin. Fold 2 opposite corners together, forming a triangle. Seal edges. Pull the right and left corners of folded triangle down and below folded edge so they slightly overlap. Moisten overlapping corners and pinch together. Fry 2 or 3 at a time in hot oil or shortening in mini-fryer about 1 to 1-1/2 minutes until crisp and golden. Drain. Serve hot. Make 25 to 35 appetizers.

Crab Won Ton

Add gourmet flavor to your meal!

1/4 lb. cooked crab meat
1 (3-oz.) pkg. cream cheese,
   room temperature
1 tablespoon soft bread crumbs
1/4 teaspoon sesame seeds

1/4 teaspoon seasoned salt
20 to 25 won ton skins or wrappers
Oil or shortening for frying
Chinese Mustard Sauce, see below
Catsup, if desired

Chinese Mustard Sauce:
2 tablespoons dry mustard
2 tablespoons water

Drain and flake crab meat. Pat with paper towels to remove as much moisture as possible. In medium bowl, combine cream cheese, bread crumbs, sesame seeds and seasoned salt. Stir in crab meat. Place about 1 teaspoon crab mixture in center of each won ton skin. Moisten edges of skin. Fold 2 opposite corners together, forming a triangle. Seal edges. Pull the right and left corners of folded triangle down and below folded edge so they slightly overlap. Moisten overlapping corners and pinch together. Drop into hot oil or shortening in mini-fryer. Fry about 1 minute, until crisp and golden. Drain. Serve with Chinese Mustard Sauce or catsup. Makes about 20 to 25 appetizers.

Chinese Mustard Sauce:
In a small bowl, combine dry mustard and water. Stir until well-blended.

Tuna Won Ton

Tempt their tastes with tuna!

1 (6-1/2-oz.) can tuna, drained
8 water chestnuts, finely chopped
2 green onions, chopped
1 tablespoon soy sauce
1/2 teaspoon sugar
1 egg, beaten
30 to 35 won ton skins or wrappers
Oil or shortening for frying

In medium bowl, flake tuna. Combine with water chestnuts, onions, soy sauce, sugar and egg. Place about 1 teaspoon tuna mixture in center of each won ton skin. Moisten edges of skin. Fold 2 opposite corners together, forming a triangle. Seal edges. Pull the right and left corners of folded triangle down and below folded edge so they slightly overlap. Moisten overlapping corners and pinch together. Fry 2 or 3 at a time in hot oil or shortening in mini-fryer about 1 minute or until crisp and golden. Drain. Serve hot. Makes 30 to 35 appetizers.

Green Cheese Balls

A super spinach idea.

1 (10-oz.) pkg. frozen spinach, thawed
2 eggs, slightly beaten
1-1/2 cups fine dry bread crumbs
1/2 teaspoon salt
1/2 teaspoon seasoned salt
1 teaspoon grated onion
1/2 cup grated Cheddar cheese
Dash nutmeg
Oil or shortening for frying
Hollandaise or tomato sauce, if desired

Drain and squeeze spinach to remove all water. Finely chop spinach and place in large bowl. Add eggs, bread crumbs, salt, seasoned salt, onion, grated Cheddar cheese and nutmeg. Shape into 3/4- to 1-inch balls. Drop into hot oil or shortening in mini-fryer. Fry until brown. Drain. Serve hot. Good plain, or with Hollandaise or tomato sauce, if desired. Makes 20 to 25 appetizers.

Dallas Dippers

Giant puffy disks with a super South-of-the-Border flavor.

2 cups biscuit mix
1/2 cup cold water
1 teaspoon chili powder

Cornmeal
Oil or shortening for frying
Guacamole sauce, if desired

In medium bowl, combine biscuit mix, water and chili powder to form soft dough. On a lightly floured board, knead 5 times. Divide into 16 equal parts. Shape each into a ball on board sprinkled with cornmeal. Roll each ball into a 4-inch circle. Drop circles into hot oil or shortening in mini-fryer. Fry until puffy and golden. Drain and serve warm or cool. Serve as snacks or as dippers for guacamole or your favorite dip. Makes 16 appetizers.

Mini Chicken-Almond Turnovers

Rich and flaky pastry with delicious chicken filling.

Chicken-Almond Filling, see below
1 cup flour
1/2 teaspoon salt

2/3 cup heavy cream
Oil or shortening for frying

Chicken-Almond Filling:
1 (4-3/4-oz.) can chicken spread
2 tablespoons chopped blanched almonds

1 egg, hard-cooked, peeled and chopped
1 tablespoon imitation bacon bits

Make Chicken-Almond Filling and set aside. In medium bowl, combine flour and salt; stir in cream to make stiff dough. On lightly floured board, roll out about 1/8-inch thick. Cut into 2-inch circles. Place about 1 teaspoon Chicken-Almond Filling in center of each. Fold over and press edges together. Fry in hot oil or shortening in mini-fryer about 1-1/2 to 2 minutes until golden brown. Drain. Serve warm or cool. Makes 30 appetizers.

Chicken-Almond Filling:
Combine chicken spread, almonds, egg and bacon bits. Blend well.

Miniature Chilies Rellenos

Puffy batter around cheese and chilies.

1 (4-oz.) can whole green chilies
1/4 lb. Monterey Jack cheese
1 tablespoon flour
2 eggs, separated

1/8 teaspoon salt
2 tablespoons flour
Oil or shortening for frying
Salsa or taco sauce, if desired

Drain chilies and discard seeds. Cut into 12 strips. Cut Monterey Jack cheese into 12 cubes. Wrap a chili strip around each cheese cube. Roll in 1 tablespoon flour. In medium bowl, beat egg whites until soft peaks form. In small bowl, beat egg yolks and salt until thick. Stir 2 tablespoons flour into beaten yolks. Fold yolk mixture into beaten egg whites. Coat each chili-cheese cube with egg mixture. Fry 3 cubes at a time in hot oil or shortening in mini-fryer about 5 minutes or until done. Drain and serve hot. Good plain or with salsa or taco sauce, if desired. Makes 12 appetizers.

Toasty Shrimp Rolls

Roll up shrimp in bread!

1/2 lb. uncooked medium shrimp
1/4 cup butter, softened
1 teaspoon dried dill weed
1/4 teaspoon seasoned salt

1/8 teaspoon pepper
10 or 11 thin slices bread
Oil or shortening for frying

Shell shrimp. Cut slit lengthwise along vein but not completely through; remove vein. Pat dry. Spread shrimp as flat as possible in butterfly fashion. In small bowl, combine butter with dill weed, seasoned salt and pepper. Spread on shrimp. Trim crusts from bread. Cut each slice in half. Flatten bread with rolling pin. Place 1 shrimp on each 1/2 slice of bread. Roll up bread and shrimp from broad side of shrimp to tail. Secure with toothpick. Chill at least 1 hour. Carefully drop shrimp rolls into hot oil or shortening in mini-fryer. Fry 1 to 2 minutes, until golden. Drain, serve hot. Makes 20 to 22 appetizers.

Doughnuts

Doughnuts are favorites, everywhere! They are a form of fried cake or bread. Cake doughnuts are made of flour, milk, eggs and seasonings, with a leavening agent of baking powder and/or baking soda. The leavening ingredients, in addition to the eggs, make doughnuts puff up when they are in hot oil or shortening. Bread doughnuts are made with yeast. This kind usually takes longer to make because you have to wait for the yeast to "work."

Naturally, most of the recipes in this section are doughnuts with the typical round shape and a hole in the center. However, some that use the traditional ingredients are dropped from a spoon rather than rolled and cut out. When making drop doughnuts, try to make the approximate size indicated in the recipe. If they are too large, the outside browns too much before the center is done.

Don't be afraid to try even if you've never made doughnuts before. Read through the recipe, making sure you have all ingredients on hand. Then follow the directions, being careful to measure accurately. I find that the flour measurement is most accurate when I spoon the flour from the canister (or from the bag of flour) into a measuring cup. Then level off the cup with a spatula. For most cake-type doughnuts, it is easier to roll out the dough if you chill it for an hour or two ahead of time. After rolling out the dough, and cutting out the doughnuts, let them stand 10 to 15 minutes, if possible, while heating the mini-fryer. Then carefully lift each doughnut with a pancake turner and gently lower it into the hot oil or shortening in the mini-fryer. Fry it the approximate time indicated in the recipe.

For yeast doughnuts, most recipes allow a slight variation in the amount of flour. Use the amount that makes the dough easy for you to handle. Follow the suggested times for the dough to double, but check it occasionally. When the yeast doughnuts are ready to be fried, lift them carefully to keep their nice round shape.

For glazed doughnuts, it's a good idea to dip them into the glaze while they're still warm. For sugar-coating, wait until they're almost cool before dipping them or shaking them in a plastic bag with sugar.

Spiced Raisin Balls

A quick, spicy doughnut fillled with raisins and pecans.

2 cups flour
1/4 cup sugar
1 tablespoon baking powder
1 teaspoon cinnamon
1/4 teaspoon ground cloves
1 teaspoon salt
1 egg, beaten

3/4 cup milk
1/4 cup cooking oil
1/4 cup coarsely chopped pecans
1/4 cup raisins
Oil or shortening for frying
Sugar, if desired

In large bowl, stir together flour, 1/4 cup sugar, baking powder, cinnamon, cloves and salt. In medium bowl, combine egg, milk, and 1/4 cup oil. Stir into dry ingredients until moistened. Stir in pecans and raisins. Drop by teaspoons into hot oil or shortening in mini-fryer. Fry until brown, about 2-1/2 to 3 minutes. Drain. Roll in sugar, if desired. Makes 25 to 30 balls.

Buttermilk Doughnuts

Delicious plain, sprinkled with sugar or glazed.

1 egg
1/2 cup sugar
1/2 cup buttermilk
1/2 teaspoon vanilla
2 cups flour
1-1/2 teaspoons baking powder

1/4 teaspoon baking soda
1/4 teaspoon salt
1/4 teaspoon ground ginger
1/2 teaspoon mace
Oil or shortening for frying
Glaze, see below

Glaze:
1/2 cup sifted powdered sugar
1 tablespoon warm milk

In medium bowl, beat egg until light and foamy. Beat in sugar. Add buttermilk and vanilla. Mix in flour, baking powder, baking soda, salt, ginger and mace. Chill about 1 hour. On lightly floured board, pat out dough 3/4-inch thick. Cut with floured doughnut cutter. Carefully drop into hot oil or shortening in mini-fryer. Fry about 2 to 2-1/2 minutes or until golden brown. Drain. Dip top of warm doughnuts into glaze. Place doughnuts glaze-side-up on rack. Makes 8 or 9 doughnuts.

Glaze:
Combine 1/2 cup powdered sugar and 1 tablespoon warm milk. Blend until smooth.

Old-Fashioned Potato Doughnuts

Moist and flavorful on the inside, crunchy on the outside.

1-1/2 cups flour
1/3 cup sugar
1 tablespoon baking powder
1/4 teaspoon nutmeg
1/4 teaspoon salt
1/2 cup prepared mashed potatoes

2 tablespoon butter or margarine
1 egg
2 tablespoons milk
1/2 teaspoon vanilla
Oil or shortening for frying
Sifted powdered sugar

In medium bowl, combine flour with sugar, baking powder, nutmeg and salt. With pastry blender or fork, cut in mashed potatoes and butter or margarine until mixture resembles coarse crumbs. In small bowl, mix egg, milk and vanilla. Stir into flour mixture. Knead on lightly floured board. Roll out about 1/2-inch thick. Cut with floured doughnut cutter. Drop into hot oil or shortening in mini-fryer. Fry about 2 minutes, until golden brown. Drain and cool. Sprinkle with powdered sugar. Makes 8 or 9 doughnuts.

Churros

So delicate and crisp, they look like ruffled ribbons.

1/4 cup water
1/16 teaspoon salt
1/4 teaspoon sugar
2 tablespoons butter or margarine
1/4 cup flour

1 egg
1/4 teaspoon vanilla
Oil or shortening for frying
Sifted powdered sugar

In medium saucepan, combine water, salt, sugar and butter or margarine. Heat until butter or margarine melts. Bring to full boil over medium-high heat. Add flour all at once. Remove from heat and beat with a spoon until it forms thick paste that separates from sides of pan. Add egg, beating until smooth and shiny. Stir in vanilla. Let cool 15 minutes. Heat oil or shortening in mini-fryer. Fill a large pastry bag or cookie press, fitted with large star tip, with 1/2 the mixture. Squeeze mixture into hot oil to form a ribbon 4 to 5 inches long. Cut off with a knife. Fry until golden brown. Repeat with remaining dough. Drain and sprinkle with powdered sugar. Serve warm. Makes 22 to 25 churros.

Variation:
Slightly crush 1 teaspoon anise seed and combine with 1/2 cup sifted powdered sugar. Cover and let stand several hours. Sift; discard seeds. Sprinkle on hot churros.

Old-Fashioned Doughnuts

Dress up this basic cake doughnut recipe with your favorite frosting.

1 egg
1/2 cup sugar
2 cups flour
2 teaspoons baking powder
1/2 teaspoon salt

1 tablespoon melted butter
1/3 cup milk
1/2 teaspoon vanilla
Oil or shortening for frying
Sugar or frosting, if desired

In large bowl, beat egg until light and lemon-colored. Gradually beat in sugar until thick. In medium bowl, combine flour, baking powder and salt. Add dry ingredients alternately with melted butter, milk and vanilla to egg mixture. Stir until flour is moistened. If dough is hard to handle, chill for 1 hour. On lightly floured board, roll out about 1/2-inch thick. Cut with floured doughnut cutter. Fry in hot oil or shortening in mini-fryer about 1 minute on each side, or until golden brown. Drain. Sprinkle with sugar, or frost, if desired. Makes 8 to 10 doughnuts.

Harvest Doughnuts

Apple butter provides the spicy flavor.

2 cups biscuit mix
2 tablespoons sugar
1 egg, beaten
1/2 cup apple butter

1 teaspoon vanilla
Oil or shortening for frying
Apple-Butter Glaze, see below
1/2 cup chopped walnuts

Apple-Butter Glaze:
1-1/2 cups sifted powdered sugar
2 tablespoons milk

1-1/2 tablespoons apple butter

In large bowl, combine biscuit mix and sugar. In small bowl, mix egg, 1/2 cup apple butter and vanilla. Add to dry ingredients. Mix until smooth. Cover; chill thoroughly. On lightly floured board, knead dough 8 to 10 times. Roll out about 1/4-inch thick. Cut with floured doughnut cutter. Fry in hot oil or shortening in mini-fryer for 1 to 1-1/2 minutes until brown. Drain. Dip warm doughnuts in Apple-Butter Glaze and then in walnuts. Makes 8 to 10 doughnuts.

Apple-Butter Glaze:
Combine powdered sugar, milk and 1-1/2 tablespoons apple butter. Mix well.

Old-Fashioned Doughnuts

How to Make
Spicy Orange Puffs

Make a well in center of dry ingredients for orange juice and milk.

Holding a batter-filled teaspoon over the hot oil, push into mini-fryer with another teaspoon.

With tongs, roll cooked puffs in sugar-cinnamon mixture before serving.

Sour-Cream Doughnuts

Firm-textured and flavorful.

1 egg
1/2 cup sugar
1/3 cup dairy sour cream
1-1/2 cups flour
1/2 teaspoon baking soda

1 teaspoon baking powder
1/8 teaspoon nutmeg
1/8 teaspoon salt
Oil or shortening for frying
Sugar or frosting, if desired

In large bowl, beat egg; gradually beat in sugar. Stir in sour cream. In medium bowl, combine flour, baking soda, baking powder, nutmeg and salt. Fold into egg mixture; stir until smooth. Chill dough about an hour. On lightly floured board, roll out about 3/8-inch thick. Cut with floured doughnut cutter. Fry, 1 or 2 at a time, in hot oil or shortening in mini-fryer about 2 minutes or until golden brown. Drain. Serve plain, sprinkle with sugar, or frost, if desired. Makes 8 to 10 doughnuts.

Spicy Orange Puffs

So spicy and crunchy!

2 cups flour
1/4 cup sugar
3 teaspoons baking powder
1/2 teaspoon salt
1/2 teaspoon nutmeg
1/4 cup cooking oil
1/2 cup milk

1/4 cup orange juice
1/2 teaspoon grated orange peel
1 egg, slightly beaten
Oil or shortening for frying
1/3 cup sugar
1/2 teaspoon cinnamon

In medium bowl, combine flour, sugar, baking powder, salt and nutmeg. Make a well in center. Pour in 1/4 cup oil, milk, orange juice, grated orange peel and egg. Stir until well-mixed. Drop slightly-rounded teaspoons of batter into hot oil or shortening in mini-fryer. Larger puffs do not cook well in center. Fry about 2-1/2 to 3 minutes or until brown. Drain. Roll in 1/3 cup sugar mixed with cinnamon. Makes 28 to 30 puffs.

Calas

Our version of the famous New Orleans rice doughnut.

1 egg
1/4 cup sugar
2 cups cold, *cooked* rice
   short or medium grain
1/2 cup flour
1-1/2 teaspoons baking powder

1/4 teaspoon salt
1/2 teaspoon cinnamon
1/4 teaspoon ground cloves
1/4 teaspoon nutmeg
Oil or shortening for frying
Sifted powdered sugar

In large bowl, beat egg and sugar until light and thick. Mix in cooked rice, flour, baking powder, salt, cinnamon, cloves and nutmeg. Drop by teaspoon into hot oil or shortening in mini-fryer. Fry about 2 minutes or until golden. Drain. Sprinkle with powdered sugar. Serve hot. Makes 20 to 24 calas.

Double-Orange Doughnuts

For those who love that real orange flavor!

3-1/4 cups flour
2 teaspoons baking powder
2 eggs, beaten
2/3 cup sugar
1 teaspoon vanilla

1 teaspoon grated orange peel
2/3 cup orange juice
1/4 cup butter or margarine, melted
Oil or shortening for frying
Orange Glaze, see below

Orange Glaze:
2 cups sifted powdered sugar
1 teaspoons grated orange peel

3 tablespoons orange juice

In medium bowl, stir together flour and baking powder. In large bowl, beat eggs, sugar and vanilla together until thick and lemon-colored. In small bowl, combine grated orange peel, orange juice and melted butter or margarine. Add orange mixture and 3/4 of dry ingredients alternately to egg mixture. Beat with electric mixer just until blended after each addition. Stir in remaining dry ingredients by hand. Cover; chill dough for 2 hours. On lightly floured board, roll out about 3/8-inch thick. Cut with floured doughnut cutter. Fry in hot oil or shortening in mini-fryer about 1 minute on each side. Drain. While warm, drizzle with Orange Glaze. Makes 16 doughnuts.

Orange Glaze:
Combine powdered sugar, grated orange peel and orange juice. Stir until well-blended.

Mincemeat Doughnuts

Perfect for a holiday brunch.

2 cups flour
2 teaspoons baking powder
1/2 teaspoon salt
1 tablespoon butter or margarine,
  softened
1/4 cup corn syrup

1 teaspoon grated lemon peel
1 egg, beaten
1 cup mincemeat
Oil or shortening for frying
Sifted powdered sugar

In medium bowl, combine flour, baking powder and salt. In large bowl, mix softened butter or margarine, corn syrup, grated lemon peel and egg. Add mincemeat. Stir in flour mixture. Chill for 1 hour. On lightly floured board, roll out about 1/2-inch thick. Carefully cut with floured doughnut cutter. Some of the fruit pieces may be hard to cut. Fry in hot oil or shortening in mini-fryer for about 2 to 2-1/2 minutes or until golden brown. Drain. Sprinkle with powdered sugar. Makes 10 to 12 doughnuts.

Double-Chocolate Doughnuts

A dream-come-true for chocolate lovers!

1 egg
1/2 cup sugar
1 (1-oz.) square unsweetened chocolate
1 tablespoon butter or margarine
1/2 cup mashed potatoes
1-3/4 cups flour

3 teaspoons baking powder
1/2 teaspoon salt
1/3 cup milk
Oil or shortening for frying
Chocolate Frosting, see below

Chocolate Frosting:
2 tablespoons butter or margarine
1 (1-oz.) square unsweetened chocolate
1 cup sifted powdered sugar

2 tablespoons boiling water
1/4 teaspoon vanilla

In a large bowl, beat egg until light. Beat in sugar. Melt unsweetened chocolate and butter or margarine together; add to egg mixture. Stir in potatoes. Mix flour, baking powder and salt. Add milk alternately with flour mixture. Chill for 1 hour. On lightly floured board, roll out about 3/8-inch thick. Cut with floured doughnut cutter. Fry in hot oil or shortening in mini-fryer about 2 minutes or until crusty brown. Drain. Cool and coat with Chocolate Frosting. Makes 12 to 14 doughnuts.

Chocolate Frosting:
Melt butter or margarine and unsweetened chocolate. Beat in powdered sugar, boiling water and vanilla. Mix well.

Chocolate-Cinnamon Doughnuts

For those whose favorite flavor is chocolate.

2/3 cup sugar
1 egg beaten
2 tablespoons butter or margarine, softened
1/2 teaspoon vanilla
2 cups flour
3 tablespoons unsweetened cocoa powder
2 teaspoons baking powder

1/8 teaspoon baking soda
1/2 teaspoon cinnamon
1/2 teaspoon salt
1/3 cup buttermilk
Oil or shortening for frying
Cocoa glaze, see below

Cocoa Glaze:
1 cup sifted powdered sugar
1 tablespoon unsweetened cocoa powder

1/2 tablespoon butter, softened
1-1/2 tablespoons boiling water

In large bowl, gradually add sugar to egg, beating until thick and lemon-colored. Stir in softened butter or margarine and vanilla. In medium bowl, combine flour, cocoa powder, baking powder, baking soda, cinnamon and salt. Stir into egg mixture alternately with buttermilk. Chill about 2 hours. Dough will be slightly sticky. On lightly floured board, roll out *half* the dough at a time about 1/2-inch thick. Keep remaining dough chilled. Cut with floured doughnut cutter. Repeat with remaining dough. Fry in hot oil or shortening in mini-fryer for 2 minutes. Drain. Dip top of warm doughnuts into Cocoa Glaze. Makes 8 to 10 doughnuts.

Cocoa Glaze:
Combine powdered sugar, cocoa powder, softened butter and boiling water. Stir until smooth.

Beignets (New Orleans Doughnuts)

So light and fluffy—like those from the French Quarter.

1 pkg. dry yeast
3/4 cup warm water
    (about 110°F, 43°C)
1/4 cup sugar
1/2 teaspoon salt

1 egg
1/2 cup evaporated milk, undiluted
3-1/2 to 4 cups flour
Oil or shortening for frying
Powdered sugar

In large bowl, dissolve yeast in water. Add sugar, salt, egg and evaporated milk. Gradually stir in 2 cups of the flour. Beat until smooth. Add remaining flour, 1/3 cup at a time, beating to form a smooth, firm dough. Cover and refrigerate overnight. On lightly floured board, roll out dough about 3/8-inch thick, adding more flour if necessary. Cut in 2" x 3" rectangles or diamonds. Drop in hot oil or shortening in mini-fryer about 1 to 2 minutes or until golden brown. Drain. Sprinkle with powdered sugar. Makes 22 to 26 beignets.

Raised Potato Doughnuts

Light, puffy and wonderful.

1 pkg. dry yeast
1/4 cup warm water
  (about 110°F, 43°C)
1/2 cup milk
2 tablespoons butter or margarine
1/4 cup sugar

1/2 cup mashed potatoes
1 egg
3/4 teaspoon salt
2-3/4 to 3-1/4 cups flour
Oil or shortening for frying
Sugar, if desired

Combine dry yeast with warm water and set aside. In small saucepan, heat milk with butter or margarine and sugar until butter or margarine begins to melt; cool to lukewarm. In large bowl, combine mashed potatoes with egg. Stir in cooled milk mixture, dissolve yeast and salt. Gradually beat in flour to make a soft dough. Turn out on lightly floured board; knead until smooth. Place in lightly buttered bowl, turn dough to butter top. Cover. Let rise in a warm place for 1 to 1-1/2 hours or until doubled in bulk. Punch down; knead again; and on lightly floured board, roll out about 1/4-inch thick. Cut with floured doughnut cutter. Cover and let rise until doubled, in bulk. Carefully drop into hot oil or shortening in mini-fryer. Fry about 2 minutes or until brown. Drain. Sprinkle with sugar, if desired. Makes 18 to 20 doughnuts.

Spicy Raised Doughnuts

So nice and spicy!

1 pkg. dry yeast
1 cup flour
1 teaspoon nutmeg
1/2 teaspoon cinnamon
1 cup milk
2 tablespoons sugar
1 teaspoon salt

2 tablespoons butter or margarine
1/2 cup flour
1 egg
1 cup flour
Oil or shortening for frying
Sugar or frosting, if desired

In medium bowl, combine dry yeast with 1 cup flour, nutmeg and cinnamon. In small saucepan, heat milk, sugar, salt and butter or margarine over low heat until very warm, 120°F to 130°F (49°C to 54°C). Add warm-milk mixture to dry ingredients. Beat for 2 minutes at medium speed, scraping bowl occasionally. Add 1/2 cup flour and egg. Beat at high speed for 2 minutes, scraping bowl occasionally. Stir in 1 cup flour and mix well. Cover and let rise in a warm place until doubled in bulk. Turn out on lightly floured board; shape into a soft ball. Roll out about 1/2-inch thick; let rise 20 minutes. Cut with floured doughnut cutter. With slotted spoon or pancake turner, carefully drop 1 or 2 doughnuts at a time into hot oil or shortening in mini-fryer. Fry about 2 minutes or until golden brown. Drain. Serve plain, sprinkle with sugar, or frost, if desired. Makes 12 doughnuts.

Dutch Doughnuts

Holland's traditional New Year's treat.

1 pkg. dry yeast
1/4 cup warm water
  (about 110°F, 43°C)
1/2 cup milk
1/4 cup sugar
2-1/4 cups flour
1/2 teaspoon salt
1/2 teaspoon grated lemon peel

2 eggs
1 large cooking apple, cored,
  peeled and chopped
1/2 cup currants
1/2 cup raisins
Oil or shortening for frying
1/2 cup sugar
1 teaspoon cinnamon

In large bowl, combine yeast and water. Let stand several minutes, then add milk. In medium bowl, mix 1/4 cup sugar with flour, salt and grated lemon peel. Add 1/2 the flour mixture to liquid mixture, beating until well-blended. Add eggs, one at a time, beating after each. Beat in remaining flour mixture. Stir in apple, currants and raisins. Cover and let rise in a warm place until doubled in bulk, about 1-1/2 hours. Drop by tablespoons into hot oil or shortening in mini-fryer. Fry about 3 minutes or until brown. Drain. Dip in 1/2 cup sugar mixed with cinnamon. Makes 20 to 24 doughnuts.

Fried Cinnamon Buns

Sugar and spice—that's what these buns are made of.

3/4 cup milk
1/4 cup sugar
1 teaspoon salt
1/4 cup butter or margarine
1/4 cup warm water
  (about 110°F, 43°C)

1 pkg. dry yeast
1 egg, beaten
3 to 3-1/2 cups flour
3/4 cup sugar
1 teaspoon cinnamon
Oil or shortening for frying

In small saucepan, heat milk with 1/4 cup sugar, salt and butter or margarine until butter or margarine begins to melt. Cool to lukewarm. Mix warm water with dry yeast; stir to dissolve. In large bowl, combine dissolved yeast mixture with milk mixture, egg and 1-1/2 cups of the flour. Beat until smooth. Add more flour to make dough stiff. Knead on lightly floured board until smooth and elastic, about 6 to 8 minutes. Place in lightly buttered bowl, turning to butter top. Cover and let rise in a warm place until doubled in bulk, about 1 hour. Butter cookie sheets. Combine 3/4 cup sugar and cinnamon. Punch down dough and divide in half. Roll out each 1/2 to a 14" x 9" rectangle. Sprinkle each with 1/2 the sugar-cinnamon mixture. Roll up tightly to form two 9-inch-long rolls. Press to seal seam. Cut each roll crosswise into 9 equal pieces. Place on buttered cookie sheet, cut side up. Press down lightly to flatten rolls. Cover and let rise in a warm place until doubled in bulk, about 30 minutes. Gently drop into hot oil or shortening in mini-fryer. Fry about 2 to 3 minutes or until golden brown. If some of sugar cinnamon mixture oozes out into the oil, scoop it off oil surface with a long spoon; any remaining will solidify when oil cools, and can be strained out. Makes 18 buns.

Quickie Bismarcks

Children enjoy filling the holes with jelly.

1 (8-oz.) pkg. refrigerated biscuits
Oil or shortening for frying

Grape jelly
Sifted powdered sugar

Separate biscuits. Drop into hot oil or shortening in mini-fryer. Fry about 2 minutes or until golden. Drain. While still warm, make a slit in center of doughnut side with a paring knife. Wiggle knife slightly to make a hole about 3/4 way through each doughnut. Push 1/4 teaspoon jelly into hole. Roll in powdered sugar. Makes 10 bismarcks.

Orange-Blossom Doughnuts

One of our favorites!

3/4 cup flour
1 tablespoon sugar
1/2 teaspoon salt
1 pkg. dry yeast
1/2 cup milk
2 tablespoons water

1 tablespoon butter or margarine
1 egg
3/4 to 1 cup flour
Oil or shortening for frying
Honey-Orange Sauce, see below

Honey-Orange Sauce:
2/3 cup honey
1/3 cup orange juice

1/2 teaspoon grated orange peel

In medium bowl, thoroughly combine 3/4 cup flour, sugar, salt and yeast. In small saucepan, heat milk, water and butter or margarine until butter or margarine begins to melt, about 120°F to 130°F (49°C to 54°C). Gradually add to dry ingredients. Beat 2 minutes with electric mixer. Add egg and 1/2 cup of the flour. Beat until smooth. Stir in enough additional flour to make stiff batter. It will be consistency of a thick *batter*, not a dough. Cover; let rise in warm place until doubled in bulk, or about 1 hour. Stir down. Drop by teaspoon into hot oil or shortening in mini-fryer. Fry about 2 to 2-1/2 minutes, or until golden brown. Drain. While warm, dip into chilled Honey-Orange Sauce. Drain on wire racks. Makes 18 to 20 doughnuts.

Honey-Orange Sauce:
In small saucepan, combine honey, orange juice and grated orange peel. Heat, stirring until well-blended. Chill several hours.

Glazed Yeast Doughnuts

Better than those you buy at the bakery!

1 pkg. dry yeast
1/4 cup warm water
  (about 110°F, 43°C)
1/4 cup sugar
2 tablespoons butter or margarine
1/2 teaspoon salt

1 cup milk
2 cups flour
1 egg, well beaten
1 to 1-1/2 cups flour
Oil or shortening for frying
Vanilla Glaze, see below

Vanilla Glaze:
1 cup sifted powdered sugar
2 tablespoons milk

1/8 teaspoon vanilla

In small bowl, dissolve yeast in warm water; set aside. In saucepan, heat sugar, butter or margarine, salt and milk until butter or margarine melts. Cool to lukewarm. Pour into large mixing bowl and stir in 1/2 cup flour. Beat until smooth. Stir in dissolved yeast. Add 1-1/2 cups flour; beat until smooth. Stir in egg. Add 1 to 1-1/2 cups additional flour to make a soft dough. Turn out on lightly floured board. Cover and let stand 5 minutes. Knead about 5 minutes. Place in lightly buttered bowl. Turn dough to butter top. Cover and let rise in warm place until doubled in bulk about 1-1/2 to 2 hours. Punch down. Turn out on lightly floured board. Roll out dough about 1/4-inch thick. Cut with floured cutter into doughnut shapes or 2-inch diamonds. Cover and let rise again until doubled in bulk, about 1 hour. Fry in hot oil or shortening in mini-fryer for 1 to 1-1/2 minutes or until golden brown. Drain. Dip top of warm doughnuts in Vanilla Glaze. Place doughnuts glaze-side-up on rack. Makes 25 to 30 doughnuts.

Vanilla Glaze:
Combine powdered sugar with milk and vanilla. Blend well.

After mixing ingredients, knead dough and place in lightly buttered bowl. Cover and let rise in a warm place until the dough doubles its original size.

On lightly floured board roll out dough almost 1/4-inch thick. Cut with doughnut cutter, then cover with wax paper or clean cloth and let rise again.

How to Make Glazed Yeast Doughnuts

To prevent stretching dough out of shape, carefully slide pancake turner under each raised doughnut and gently slide it into hot oil or shortening.

Fry doughnuts until golden brown. Drain on paper towels. While still warm, dip in glaze. Place on cooling rack.

Shortcut Raised Doughnuts

Hot-roll mix saves you time and effort.

1 (13-3/4-oz.) pkg. hot-roll mix
1/2 cup warm water
  (about 110°F, 43°C)
2 egg yolks
1/2 cup dairy sour cream
1/2 teaspoon grated lemon peel

1/2 teaspoon nutmeg
3 tablespoons sugar
Oil or shortening for frying
Sugar, if desired

In large bowl, dissolve package of yeast from the hot-roll mix in warm water. Stir in egg yolks, sour cream, grated lemon peel, nutmeg and sugar. Add dry hot-roll mix; beat until well-blended. Cover and let rise in warm place for 45 to 60 minutes, or until doubled in bulk. On lightly floured board, roll out 3/8-inch to 1/2-inch thick. Cut with floured doughnut cutter. Cover and let rise about 1/2 hour or until doubled in bulk. Fry, 1 or 2 at a time, in hot oil or shortening in mini-fryer about 1-1/2 to 2 minutes, or until golden brown. Drain. Coat with sugar, if desired. Makes 14 to 16 doughnuts.

Old-Fashioned Jelly Doughnuts

A favorite for kids of all ages.

1/4 cup milk
2 tablespoons sugar
1/2 teaspoon salt
3 tablespoons butter
1 pkg. dry yeast
1/4 cup warm water
  (about 110°F, 43°C)

2 egg yolks
2 cups flour
Jam or jelly
1 egg white
Oil or shortening for frying
Sugar

In small saucepan, heat milk, 2 tablespoons sugar, salt and butter until butter begins to melt. Remove from heat and cool to lukewarm. In large bowl, sprinkle yeast over warm water. Stir until dissolved. Add cooled milk mixture, egg yolks and 1 cup of the flour. With electric mixer, beat until smooth, about 2 minutes. With wooden spoon or with hands, blend in remaining flour. Cover and let rise in a warm place until doubled in bulk, about 1-1/2 hours. Punch down dough. Turn out on lightly floured board; knead 10 minutes or until dough is smooth. Roll out 1/2 of dough about 1/4-inch thick. Cut into 6 (3-inch) rounds. Place 1 teaspoon jam or jelly in center of each round. Brush edges with egg white. Roll out remaining dough and cut into another 6 rounds. Place on top of jam- or jelly-filled rounds. Press edges to seal. Place on lightly floured cookie sheet, cover with towel and let rise until doubled in bulk, about 1 hour. Gently drop doughnuts in hot oil or shortening in mini-fryer. Fry 2-1/2 to 3 minutes or until brown, turning once. Drain. Sprinkle with sugar while warm. Makes 6 jelly doughnuts.

Apple Drop Doughnuts

No rolling out! Just drop into mini-fryer.

1/2 cup milk
1/4 cup butter or margarine
1/4 cup sugar
1 pkg. dry yeast
1/4 cup warm water
  (about 110°F, 43°C)
2 eggs
2-1/4 cups flour

1/2 teaspoon salt
1/2 teaspoon grated lemon peel
1 cooking apple, cored, peeled,
  and finely chopped
1 cup raisins or chopped dates
Oil or shortening for frying
1/2 cup sugar
1 teaspoon cinnamon

In small saucepan, heat milk, butter or margarine and sugar until butter or margarine melts; set aside to cool. In large bowl, dissolve yeast in warm water. Mix in cooled milk mixture and beat in eggs. In medium bowl, combine flour, salt and grated lemon peel. Add half the flour mixture to liquid mixture, beating until well-blended. Beat in remaining flour. Stir in apple, raisins or dates. Cover and let rise in a warm place until doubled in bulk, about 1-1/2 hours. Heat oil or shortening in mini-fryer. Spoon slightly heaping tablespoons of dough into hot oil in mini-fryer. Fry about 2 minutes or until brown. Drain. Mix 1/2 cup sugar with cinnamon. Roll warm doughnuts in cinnamon-sugar mixture. Makes about 26 to 28 drop doughnuts.

Banana Doughnuts

If you like bananas, you'll love these doughnuts!

1-1/2 cups flour
1 pkg. dry yeast
3/4 cup milk
1/3 cup shortening
1/4 cup sugar
3/4 teaspoon salt

1 egg
1/2 teaspoon grated lemon peel
1/2 cup mashed ripe banana (1 small banana)
2 to 2-1/2 cups flour
Oil or shortening for frying
Powdered sugar

In large bowl, stir together 1-1/2 cups flour and dry yeast. In small saucepan heat milk, 1/3 cup shortening, sugar and salt just until warm, 120°F to 130°F (49°C to 54°C), stirring until shortening almost melts. Add to dry mixture with egg, grated lemon peel and mashed banana. Beat with mixer on low speed for 1/2 minute, then at high speed for 3 minutes. By hand, stir in 2 to 2-1/2 cups flour or enough to make a moderately soft dough. Turn out on lightly floured board; knead until smooth and elastic, about 5 minutes. Place in lightly buttered bowl. Turn dough to butter top. Cover and let rise until doubled in bulk, about 45 to 60 minutes. Punch down. Turn out on floured surface. Roll out dough about 1/2-inch thick. Cut with floured doughnut cutter. Cover and let rise until nearly doubled in bulk, about 35 to 45 minutes. Fry in hot oil or shortening in mini-fryer about 1-1/2 to 2 minutes, or until golden brown. Drain and cool. Sprinkle with powdered sugar. Makes 18 doughnuts.

Fish & Seafood

There's no special trick to frying delicious fish and seafood. Fresh or frozen fillets of sole, cod and red snapper are really great. I like to use different kinds of coatings and a variety of sauces. These fillets make an ideal serving size and fit into mini-fryers just right when they are cut into 2- or 3-inch-long pieces. There is a lot of water around frozen fish fillets that are being thawed. Be very careful to dry frozen fish after it has completely thawed. Pour off excess water, then pat it dry with paper towels so there will be no water on the fish. Coatings are important on fish because they keep the center soft and moist, yet provide a crunchy outside layer.

Shrimp, scallops and oysters make a big hit when deep-fried. You may like to copy the popular seafood restaurants by serving your own Fisherman's Platter. You can combine fried fish fillets with shrimp and oysters or scallops. Cover all of them with the same coating or try a variety of your favorites.

Try shrimp fried in several different shapes: Traditional shrimp, with and without tails; butterflied; and fan-tailed. It isn't as complicated as it sounds. With a sharp knife and these directions, you can try several ways—and maybe even discover a new shape for shrimp.

Don't forget to look through the chapter on sauces for interesting ways to top off your favorite fried-fish and seafood dishes.

Fried Oysters

With large or small oysters, this recipe is sure to please.

1 (10-oz.) can oysters
1/3 cup flour
1/2 teaspoon salt
1/8 teaspoon pepper
1 egg, slightly beaten
1 tablespoon water

2/3 cup fine cracker crumbs
Oil or shortening for frying
Lemon wedges
Tartar Sauce, page 153, or
    Easy Seafood Sauce, page 153

Drain oysters. Pat dry with paper towels. Dip in mixture of flour, salt and pepper in shallow dish. Dip oysters in egg beaten with water in another shallow dish. Coat with cracker crumbs. Fry in hot oil or shortening in mini-fryer about 1-1/2 to 2-1/2 minutes until golden brown. Drain. Serve hot, with lemon wedges. Good with Tartar Sauce, page 153, or Easy Seafood Sauce, page 153. Makes 3 to 4 servings.

Oyster-Potato Fries

A tasty dual flavor for oyster lovers.

2 tablespoons flour
1/4 teaspoon salt
1/4 teaspoon seasoned salt
1 egg
1 teaspoon instant minced onion

2 tablespoons dairy sour cream
1 cup finely shredded potatoes
1 (10-oz.) jar or can oysters, well-drained
Oil or shortening for frying

In small bowl, combine flour, salt and seasoned salt. In medium bowl, beat egg. Stir in flour mixture, onion and sour cream. Pat potatoes dry and stir into egg-flour mixture. Pat oysters dry. Add 2 or 3 oysters at a time to potato mixture. Drop 2 or 3 coated oysters at a time by tablespoon into hot oil or shortening in mini-fryer. Fry 3 to 4 minutes or until golden brown. Drain. Serve hot. Makes 12 with large oysters, or 15 to 18 with small oysters.

Almond-Crusted Scallops

Crunchy coating makes this deep-sea favorite irresistible.

1 lb. scallops, fresh or frozen
1/4 cup soft bread crumbs
1/4 cup blanched almonds
1/2 cup flour
1/2 teaspoon salt

1/4 teaspoon pepper
1 egg, slightly beaten
2 tablespoons milk
Oil or shortening for frying

Thaw scallops, if frozen. Pat dry with paper towels. Combine bread crumbs and almonds in blender. Blend at high speed until mixture resembles fine crumbs. Set aside. In shallow dish, dip scallops in flour mixed with salt and pepper, then in small bowl, dip scallops in egg mixed with milk. Dip scallops in bread crumb-almond mixture. Drop in hot oil or shortening in mini-fryer. Fry about 1 to 2 minutes or until golden. Drain and serve hot. Makes 4 to 5 servings.

Fried Teriyaki Scallops

Marinade gives Oriental flavor to this New England favorite.

1 lb. scallops, fresh or frozen
1/2 cup soy sauce
1/4 cup white wine
2 tablespoons honey
1/2 teaspoon ground ginger

1/2 teaspoon garlic salt
1/2 cup flour
1/2 cup milk
1 cup fine cracker crumbs
Oil or shortening for frying

Thaw scallops, if frozen. Pat dry with paper towels. In medium bowl, combine soy sauce, wine, honey, ginger and garlic salt. Pour over scallops. Cover and refrigerate at least 1 hour. Drain thoroughly and pat dry. Place flour, milk and cracker crumbs separately in 3 small bowls. Dip marinated scallops in flour, then quickly in milk, and coat with cracker crumbs. Drop into hot oil or shortening in mini-fryer. Fry about 1 to 2 minutes until brown and crisp. Drain. Serve hot. Makes 4 to 5 servings.

Fried Scallops

A quick deep-sea treat.

1 lb. scallops, fresh or frozen
1/4 cup flour
1/2 teaspoon salt

1 egg, slightly beaten
1 tablespoon water
1/2 cup fine cracker or dry bread crumbs

Thaw scallops, if frozen. Pat dry with paper towels. In shallow dish, combine flour with salt. Roll scallops in flour mixture. In another small bowl, dip scallops in egg mixed with water, then coat with cracker or bread crumbs. Drop into hot oil or shortening in mini-fryer. Fry until golden, about 3 minutes. Drain. Serve hot. Makes 3 to 4 servings.

Crispy Beer-Batter Fish

Beautiful golden batter that's crispy on the outside.

1 lb. fish fillets, fresh or frozen
1 cup flour
1 teaspoon baking powder
1 teaspoon salt

1 tablespoon cooking oil
1 cup flat beer
1/4 cup flour for dipping
Oil or shortening for frying

Thaw fish, if frozen. Pat dry with paper towels. In medium mixing bowl, combine 1 cup flour, baking powder and salt. Make a well in center; pour in 1 tablespoon oil and 1 cup beer. Stir until smooth. Cut fish fillets into crosswise strips about 2 to 3 inches wide. In shallow dish, dip fish in 1/4 cup flour, then in batter. Fry in hot oil or shortening in mini-fryer about 1-1/2 minutes on each side, or until golden. Drain. Serve hot. Makes 3 to 4 servings.

Cracker-Coated Fish

Crispy coating with beautiful golden color.

1 lb. fish fillets, fresh or frozen
1/2 cup flour
1/2 teaspoon salt
1/8 teaspoon pepper
1/2 cup milk

3/4 cup finely crushed cracker crumbs
   (about 20 saltine crackers)
Oil or shortening for frying
Lemon wedges, if desired
Tartar Sauce, page 153, if desired

Thaw fish, if frozen. Pat dry with paper towels. Cut in pieces about 2 inches wide. In shallow dishes, dip fillets in flour mixed with salt and pepper, then in milk, then in cracker crumbs. Fry in hot oil or shortening in mini-fryer 2 to 3 minutes until golden. Drain. Serve with lemon wedges and Tartar Sauce, page 153, if desired. Makes 3 to 4 servings.

Butterfly Shrimp

Palate-pleasing batter and an interesting shape lend a gourmet touch.

1 lb. large uncooked shrimp	1/2 cup cold water
1 cup biscuit mix	1/2 teaspoon salt
2 eggs	Oil or shortening for frying

Shell shrimp. Cut slit lengthwise along vein, but not completely through. Remove vein. Pat dry with paper towels. In small bowl, combine biscuit mix, eggs, water and salt. Stir until smooth. Dip shrimp in batter. Fry 2 or 3 at a time in hot oil or shortening in mini-fryer about 2 to 3 minutes or until golden brown. Serve hot. Makes 3 to 4 servings.

Clockwise from top left: Cracker-Coated Fish, Crispy Beer Batter Fish, Butterfly Shrimp, Fried Scallops

How To Make Butterfly Shrimp

To butterfly shrimp, shell shrimp, leaving tails on if desired. With a sharp knife, cut lengthwise along vein, but do not cut completely through.

Remove vein. Wash shrimp and pat dry. Open in butterfly fashion, being careful not to break apart.

Fish Balls

A special idea for appetizer or entree.

1 lb. fish fillets, fresh or frozen
2 cups water
1/2 teaspoon salt
2 slices white bread, crusts removed
1/3 cup milk
1 egg, slightly beaten
1 tablespoon catsup

1 teaspoon minced instant dry onion
1/4 teaspoon seasoned salt
1/2 cup fine dry bread crumbs
Oil or shortening for frying
Tartar Sauce, page 153 or
    Sweet-Sour Sauce, page 53, if desired

Thaw fish, if frozen. Pat dry with paper towels. Heat water and salt to boiling. Add fish fillets. Simmer several minutes until fish is tender. Drain fish and flake with a fork. Tear bread in small pieces; soak in milk in medium bowl. Add flaked fish, egg, catsup, onion and seasoned salt. Shape in 1-inch balls. Roll in dry bread crumbs. Drop into hot oil or shortening in mini-fryer. Fry until golden brown, about 1 to 1-1/2 minutes. Drain and serve warm. May be served plain, or with Tartar Sauce, page 153, or Sweet-Sour Sauce, page 53. Makes 22 to 24 balls.

Shrimp With Egg Batter

Give your shrimp this thin batter coating.

1 lb. large uncooked shrimp
2 eggs
1 teaspoon sugar
1/2 teaspoon salt

1/4 teaspoon pepper
1/4 cup flour
Oil or shortening for frying

Shell shrimp. Cut slit lengthwise along vein, but not completely through. Remove vein. Pat dry with paper towels. In small bowl, beat eggs slightly. Add sugar, salt, pepper and flour. Mix well. Dip shrimp into egg mixture, drain briefly. Fry in hot oil or shortening in mini-fryer about 2-1/2 to 3 minutes or until golden. Drain and serve hot. Makes 3 to 4 servings.

Puffy Fried Shrimp

Very light and airy coating becomes crisp when fried.

1 lb. medium uncooked shrimp
1 egg, separated
1 tablespoon cooking oil
1/2 cup flat beer

3/4 cup cornstarch
1/2 teaspoon dry mustard
1/2 teaspoon salt
Oil or shortening for frying

Shell shrimp and remove vein. Pat dry with paper towels. In medium bowl, beat egg yolk with 1 tablespoon oil, and 1/2 cup beer. Combine cornstarch, dry mustard and salt. Stir into yolk mixture. In small bowl, beat egg white until stiff, but not dry. Fold into yolk mixture. Dip shrimp in batter. Fry in hot oil or shortening in mini-fryer for 2 to 3 minutes or until golden and crispy. Drain. Serve hot. Makes 3 to 4 servings.

Sweet-and-Sour Fried Shrimp

A favorite that never fails to please.

1 lb. medium uncooked shrimp
1/2 cup flour
1/4 cup cornstarch
1/2 teaspoon baking powder

1 cup water
2 tablespoons cooking oil
Oil or shortening for frying
Sweet-Sour Sauce, see below

Sweet-Sour Sauce:
1 (13-oz.) can pineapple tidbits
2 tablespoons brown sugar
1/2 teaspoon salt
1 tablespoon vinegar

1 tablespoon soy sauce
1 tablespoon cornstarch
2 tablespoons water
1 small green pepper, cut in chunks

Shell shrimp. Cut slit lengthwise along vein but not completely through. Remove vein. Pat dry with paper towels. In small bowl, combine flour, cornstarch, baking powder, water and 2 tablespoons cooking oil. Mix well. Dip shrimp in batter. Fry in hot oil or shortening in mini-fryer about 1 to 2 minutes or until golden. Drain. Serve hot with Sweet-Sour Sauce. Makes 4 to 6 servings.

Sweet-Sour Sauce:
Drain pineapple, reserving syrup. In saucepan, combine pineapple syrup with brown sugar, salt, vinegar and soy sauce. Dissolve cornstarch in water and add to syrup mixture. Cook over low heat, stirring constantly, until thickened and translucent. Stir in pineapple tidbits and green pepper. Heat through.

Tempura Platter

A complete meal, encased in lacy tempura batter.

1 lb. uncooked shrimp or fish fillets
1 green pepper
2 medium zucchini
1 onion
1 sweet potato
2 eggs, beaten

3/4 cup flour
1 cup water
1 tablespoon cornstarch
1/2 teaspoon salt
1/2 teaspoon baking powder
Oil or shortening for frying

Shell shrimp, leaving tail on. Cut slit lengthwise along vein but not completely through. Remove vein. Pat dry with paper towels. Cut fish crosswise into 2- to 3-inch pieces. Slice green pepper and zucchini. Peel and slice onion and sweet potato. In medium bowl, combine eggs with flour, water, cornstarch, salt and baking powder. Stir until well-blended, but do not beat. Dip fish and vegetables in batter immediately. Drop a few pieces at a time into hot oil or shortening in mini-fryer. Fry until golden. Drain. Serve hot. Makes 3 to 4 servings.

Fan-Tail Shrimp

Here's an interesting way to prepare shrimp with a different shape.

1 lb. large uncooked shrimp
1 cup flour
1/2 teaspoon salt
1 teaspoon sugar
1 egg, slightly beaten

1 tablespoon cooking oil
1 cup cold water
Oil or shortening for frying
Easy Seafood Sauce, page 153, if desired

Shell and devein shrimp, leaving tails on. Cut a slit through each shrimp starting about 1/2 inch from the head and running to within 1/2 inch of tail. Pull tail through slit to make fan-tailed butterfly shape. Pat dry with paper towels. In small bowl, combine flour, salt, sugar, egg, 1 tablespoon cooking oil and 1 cup cold water. Beat until almost smooth. Dip shrimp in batter and drain briefly. Fry in hot oil or shortening in mini-fryer about 2-1/2 minutes or until golden. Drain. Serve hot. Good with Easy Seafood Sauce, page 153. Makes 3 to 4 servings.

Fan-Tail Shrimp

Country-Fried Fish

A thin crunchy coating that's easy to prepare.

1 lb. fish fillets, fresh or frozen
1/3 cup evaporated milk, undiluted
3/4 cup fine cracker crumbs
1-1/2 teaspoons salt

1/8 teaspoon pepper
Oil or shortening for frying
Tartar Sauce, page 153, if desired

Thaw fish, if frozen. Pat dry with paper towels. Cut fillets crosswise into 2- to 3-inch pieces. In shallow dish, dip fish in evaporated milk, then in another dish dip in cracker crumbs mixed with salt and pepper. Carefully drop into hot oil or shortening in mini-fryer. Fry about 1-1/2 to 2 minutes until golden. Serve hot. Especially good with Tartar Sauce, page 153. Makes 4 servings.

Southern-Fried Fish

A crunchy cornmeal coating.

1 lb. fish fillets, fresh or frozen
1 egg, slightly beaten
2 tablespoons milk

1/2 cup cornmeal
1/2 teaspoon salt
Oil or shortening for frying

Thaw fish, if frozen. Pat dry with paper towels. Combine egg and milk in piepan. Mix cornmeal and salt in another piepan. Dip fish in egg mixture, then in cornmeal. Drop into hot oil or shortening in mini-fryer. Fry about 2 minutes on each side until golden brown. Drain. Serve hot. Makes 3 to 4 servings.

Crispy Fish Fillets

A thin crisp coating for your favorite fish fillets.

1 lb. fish fillets, fresh or frozen
1 egg, slightly beaten
1 tablespoon water

3/4 cup fine cracker crumbs
Oil or shortening for frying

Thaw fish, if frozen. Pat dry with paper towels. Cut into serving-size pieces. In shallow dishes, dip fish in egg mixed with water, then in cracker crumbs. Drop into hot oil or shortening in mini-fryer. Fry about 2 minutes on each side until brown and fish flakes easily with fork. Drain. Serve hot. Makes 3 to 4 servings.

Dixie Fish

For a less-concentrated cornmeal coating.

1 lb. fish fillets, fresh or frozen
1 egg
1 tablespoon water
1/2 cup flour
1/2 cup cornmeal

1/2 teaspoon salt
1/8 teaspoon pepper
Oil or shortening for frying
Lemon wedges, if desired
Tartar Sauce, page 153

Thaw fish, if frozen. Cut into pieces about 2 inches wide. Pat dry with paper towels. In shallow dish, beat egg with water. Dip fish into egg mixture, then into combination of flour, cornmeal, salt and pepper in a second dish. Fry in hot oil or shortening in mini-fryer about 2 to 3 minutes or until golden brown and fish is done in center. Drain. Serve hot with lemon wedges and Tartar Sauce, page 153, if desired. Makes 3 to 4 servings.

English-Style Fish

Make it Fish 'n Chips tonight!

1 lb. fish fillets, fresh or frozen
1/4 teaspoon salt
1/8 teaspoon pepper
1/4 cup flour

1 egg, slightly beaten
1/3 cup milk
1/3 cup flour
Oil or shortening for frying

Thaw fish, if frozen. Cut into serving-size pieces. Pat dry with paper towels. Sprinkle fish with salt and pepper. Dip in 1/4 cup flour. In shallow dish, mix egg, milk and 1/3 cup flour. Dip floured fish into batter. Fry in hot oil or shortening in mini-fryer about 3 minutes or until done. Drain. Serve hot. Makes 3 to 4 servings.

Variation:
For Fish 'n Chips, fry Kitchen French Fries, page 89. Keep potatoes warm in 250°F (121°C) oven while frying fish.

Curry-Fried Fish

Real curry fans may want to add more curry powder.

1 lb. fish fillets or shrimp, fresh or frozen
1 egg
1/4 cup milk
1/2 cup flour
1 teaspoon curry powder

1/2 teaspoon dry mustard
1/2 teaspoon salt
1/4 teaspoon paprika
1/4 teaspoon garlic salt
Oil or shortening for frying

Thaw fish, if frozen. Cut into 2-inch strips, and pat dry with paper towels. In shallow dish, beat egg with milk. In another shallow dish, combine flour with curry powder, dry mustard, salt, paprika and garlic salt. Dip fish in flour mixture, then egg-milk mixture, then again in flour mixture. Fry in hot oil or shortening in mini-fryer about 1 to 2 minutes or until crispy and golden. Drain. Serve hot. Makes 3 to 4 servings.

Walnut-Crusted Fish

Walnut coating gives an extra-special touch to fish.

1 lb. fish fillets, fresh or frozen
1/2 cup soft bread crumbs
1/2 cup walnuts
1/2 cup flour

1/2 teaspoon salt
1 egg
2 tablespoons milk
Oil or shortening for frying

Thaw fish, if frozen. Combine bread crumbs and walnuts in blender; turn on high speed and blend until mixture resembles fine crumbs. Set aside. Cut fish into strips about 2 inches wide and pat dry with paper towels. In shallow dishes, dip in flour mixed with salt, then in egg beaten with milk, then in crumb-nut mixture. Drop into hot oil or shortening in mini-fryer. Fry about 1 to 2 minutes until golden brown and crusty. Drain. Serve hot. Makes 3 to 4 servings.

Poultry

Fried chicken is no longer a tradition limited to the Southern U.S.A. When you try some of these chicken recipes, you'll want to start a similar tradition at your house, using your mini-fryer to produce golden, crunchy fried chicken.

While testing these recipes, I discovered several tips to pass along. Knowing that it takes a long time to deep-fry the thicker and larger chicken parts, I tried a variety of combinations of cooking processes. For example, when deep-fried, chicken wings came out OK, but larger pieces had a tendency to become dry and overdone on the outside before being done in the center. As a result, most recipes for chicken parts suggest that they be simmered for about 20 minutes before being fried. You can do this ahead of time, if you wish, then fry the chicken just before it is served.

The fry-bake method given in this section is convenient if you like to prepare the main dish ahead of time and heat it at the last minute. The Fry-Baked Chicken is ideal for entertaining because you can do the frying the night before; refrigerate the chicken, then put it in the oven to reheat and finish cooking while you visit with the guests. Frying gives the chicken a golden, crunchy texture that's sure to be a culinary delight.

Fried-chicken enthusiasts are divided into two groups—those who think chicken should be batter-fried and those who prefer a flour or crumb coating. Both types are included so you can take a vote at your house after you have tried them.

If everyone in your family likes the same parts of chicken, you'll be ahead if you buy a package of one kind—and avoid arguments, too! Use identical pieces instead of a whole cut-up chicken and you will get lots of applause.

Some of the smallest mini-fryers are not wide enough to accommodate very large pieces of chicken. If this is a problem, cut the large pieces in half before coating them for frying. Then cook according to directions.

Herb-Fried Chicken

Just a hint of herbs.

1 (2-1/2- to 3-lb.) frying chicken,
  cut up
4 cups chicken bouillon
1 egg
1/4 cup milk

1/2 cup flour
1/2 teaspoon fines herbes
1 teaspoon salt
1/4 teaspoon pepper
Oil or shortening for frying

In large pan, cover chicken with bouillon. Cover and simmer for 20 minutes. Drain and pat dry with paper towels; reserve bouillon for making gravy or soup, if desired. In small shallow dish, beat egg with milk. Dip chicken in egg mixture; then dip chicken in mixture of flour, fines herbes, salt and pepper. Fry 1 or 2 pieces at a time in hot oil or shortening in mini-fryer for 3 to 4 minutes, or until golden brown. Drain. Serve hot. Makes 4 servings.

Peanutty Fried Chicken

Peanut butter and chicken go great together!

1 (2-1/2- to 3-lb.) frying chicken,
  cut up
Water
1 egg, beaten
1/2 cup peanut butter
1 teaspoon salt

1/8 teaspoon pepper
2/3 cup milk
1/4 cup flour
1/2 cup fine dry bread crumbs
Oil or shortening for frying

In large pan, simmer chicken in water for about 20 minutes. Drain. Pat dry with paper towels. In small bowl, blend together egg, peanut butter, salt and pepper. Gradually stir in milk. In shallow bowl coat chicken with flour; shake off excess. Then dip into peanut-butter mixture. Drain on rack over wax paper. Coat with bread crumbs. Drop 1 or 2 pieces at a time into hot oil or shortening in mini-fryer. Cook until golden brown, about 2 minutes. Drain. Serve hot. Makes 3 to 4 servings.

Italian-Fried Chicken

Salad dressing gives chicken an Italian flavor.

1 (2-1/2- to 3-lb.) frying chicken,
   cut up
Water
3/4 cup cornmeal

1/2 pkg. (about 1/2 oz.)
   Italian salad dressing mix
1/4 cup heavy cream
Oil or shortening for frying

In large pan, cover chicken with water. Cover and simmer about 20 minutes. Drain and pat dry with paper towels. In shallow pan, combine cornmeal and dry salad mix. In a small bowl, dip chicken pieces in cream, then in cornmeal mixture. Fry in hot oil or shortening in mini-fryer for 2 to 3 minutes or until brown and crispy. Drain. Serve hot. Makes 3 to 4 servings.

Paper-Wrapped Chicken

Have you ever fried with paper?

2 cups uncooked chicken, skinned, boned
   and cut in 1-in. squares
1/2 teaspoon salt
1/2 teaspoon sugar
1 tablespoon soy sauce
1 tablespoon white wine

5 green onions,
   cut in 1/2-in. pieces
Parchment paper,
   cut in 5- or 6-in. squares
Oil or shortening for frying

In medium bowl, combine chicken with salt, sugar, soy sauce and wine. Mix well and marinate several hours. Place 2 squares of chicken and one piece of onion on each piece of parchment. Roll up and twist ends. Carefully drop, 3 or 4 at a time, into hot oil or shortening in mini-fryer. Fry about 2 minutes. Drain and serve hot. Carefully unwrap and remove parchment at the table. Makes about 30 to 35 packets.

Note:
Parchment paper can be found in gourmet shops, hardware stores and the housewares section of department stores.

Batter-Fried Chicken

A traditional batter for deep-fried chicken.

1 (2-1/2- to 3-lb.) frying chicken,
  cut up
Water, salted
1 egg, slightly beaten
2/3 cup milk

1 cup flour
1-1/2 teaspoons baking powder
1 teaspoon salt
Oil or shortening for frying

In large pan, cover chicken with salted water and simmer about 20 minutes. Drain well and pat dry with paper towels. In medium bowl, combine egg and milk; stir in flour, baking powder and salt. Beat until smooth. Dip chicken in batter. Drain on rack over wax paper. Drop 1 or 2 chicken pieces at a time into hot oil or shortening in mini-fryer. Fry about 2-1/2 to 3 minutes on each side or until brown and done inside. Drain. Serve hot. Makes 3 to 4 servings.

Spicy Batter-Fried Chicken

Crispy and nicely seasoned with a spicy coating.

1 (2-1/2- to 3-lb.) frying chicken,
  cut up
Water
1 cup flour
1 teaspoon seasoned salt
1 teaspoon paprika

1 teaspoon garlic salt
1/2 teaspoon poultry seasoning
1 teaspoon pepper
1 egg
1/2 cup milk
Oil or shortening for frying

In large pan, cover chicken with water. Bring to a boil, cover and simmer about 20 minutes. Drain thoroughly. Pat dry with paper towels. In piepan, combine flour with seasoned salt, paprika, garlic salt, poultry seasoning and pepper. In small bowl, beat egg with milk. Dip chicken in flour mixture, then in egg mixture and again in flour mixture. Drop 2 or 3 pieces at a time into hot oil or shortening in mini-fryer. Fry 3 to 4 minutes or until crispy and golden brown. Drain. Serve hot. Makes 3 to 4 servings.

Fry-Baked Chicken

Fry it now, and bake when you're ready to eat!

1 (2-1/2- to 3-lb.) frying chicken,
  cut up
1 teaspoon salt
1/8 teaspoon pepper

1 egg, slightly beaten
1/2 cup milk
1/2 cup flour
Oil or shortening for frying

Sprinkle chicken with salt and pepper. In shallow dish, combine egg and milk. Dip chicken in egg mixture, then in flour. Drop 1 or 2 pieces of chicken at a time into hot oil or shortening in mini-fryer. Fry about 2 to 3 minutes or until golden brown. Drain. Place in shallow baking dish. Bake 30 to 40 minutes in 350°F (177°C) oven. Makes 3 to 4 servings.

Sesame Chicken

The extra crunch comes from sesame seeds!

6 to 8 chicken drumsticks
Water
1 egg, slightly beaten
1/4 cup milk
1/4 cup flour

2 tablespoons sesame seeds
1/2 teaspoon salt
1/8 teaspoon pepper
Oil or shortening for frying

In pan, cover drumsticks with water. Cover and simmer 15 to 20 minutes. Drain thoroughly and pat dry with paper towels. In shallow bowl, combine egg and milk. In another shallow bowl, mix flour, sesame seeds, salt and pepper. Dip drumsticks 1 at a time in milk mixture, then in flour mixture. Cook 2 pieces at a time in hot oil or shortening in mini-fryer 3 minutes or until crisp and golden. Drain. Serve hot. Makes 3 to 4 servings.

Busy-Day Fried Chicken

Here's a good time-saving batter.

1 (2-1/2- to 3-lb.) frying chicken,
  cut up
Water, salted

1 cup pancake mix
3/4 cup water

In large pan, simmer chicken in salted water for 20 minutes. Drain well and pat dry with paper towels. In small bowl, combine pancake mix with 3/4 cup water. Beat several minutes to blend. Dip chicken in batter. Drain well on rack over wax paper. Gently drop 1 or 2 pieces of coated chicken at a time into hot oil or shortening in mini-fryer. Fry until golden brown or about 2 to 3 minutes. Drain. Serve hot. Makes 3 to 4 servings.

Crunchy Bran Chicken

You'll love this crunchy, golden chicken.

1 (2-1/2- to 3-lb.) frying chicken,
  cut up
Water, salted
1 egg, beaten
1 cup milk
1/2 cup whole bran cereal

1/4 cup cooking oil
3/4 cup flour
1 teaspoon baking powder
1/2 teaspoon seasoned salt
1/2 teaspoon onion salt
Oil or shortening for frying

In large saucepan, simmer chicken in lightly salted water for 20 minutes. Drain and pat dry with paper towels. In small bowl, combine egg, milk, cereal and 1/4 cup oil; let stand 5 minutes. In medium bowl, stir together flour, baking powder, seasoned salt and onion salt. Add egg mixture. Stir until blended. Dip chicken pieces in batter, turning to coat all sides. Drain on rack over wax paper. Drop 1 or 2 chicken pieces at a time into hot oil or shortening in mini-fryer and fry about 2 minutes or until golden brown. Drain. Serve hot. Makes 3 to 4 servings.

Bouillon-Fried Chicken

Give chicken extra flavor with bouillon coating.

1 (2-1/2- to 3-lb.) frying chicken,
   cut up
Water
1/2 cup flour
1/2 teaspoon salt
1 cup buttermilk

3/4 cup fine dry bread crumbs
1 teaspoon seasoned salt
1/4 teaspoon seasoned pepper
1/4 teaspoon celery salt
1 chicken bouillon cube, finely crushed
Oil or shortening for frying

In large pan, cover chicken with water. Bring to a boil, cover and simmer about 20 minutes. Drain and pat dry with paper towels. In 3 shallow dishes, dip chicken in flour mixed with salt; then in buttermilk; then in mixture of bread crumbs, seasoned salt, seasoned pepper, celery salt and crushed bouillon. Fry 2 or 3 pieces at a time in hot oil or shortening in mini-fryer 3 to 4 minutes or until golden brown. Drain. Serve hot. Makes 4 servings.

Chicken Kiev

The ultimate in elegance!

1/2 cup butter, softened
1 tablespoon finely chopped parsley
1 teaspoon minced chives
1/2 teaspoon tarragon
1 small clove garlic, crushed
1/2 teaspoon salt
1/8 teaspoon pepper

3 whole chicken breasts,
   skinned, boned
1/3 cup flour
1 egg, slightly beaten
1/2 cup fine dry bread crumbs
Oil or shortening for frying

In small bowl, mix butter with parsley, chives, tarragon, garlic, salt and pepper. Form into a 3-inch square. Freeze until firm. Cut chicken breasts in half. With wooden mallet, pound chicken about 1/4-inch thick, being careful not to break meat. Cut butter mixture into 6 pats . Place 1 pat in center of each piece of chicken. Bring sides and ends of chicken over butter mixture, making sure no butter mixture is showing. Fasten with toothpick. In piepan, roll each in flour. In small bowl, dip chicken in egg; then in piepan, dip chicken in bread crumbs. Refrigerate about 1 hour. Drop 2 pieces chicken at a time into hot oil or shortening in mini-fryer. Fry until browned, about 6 minutes. Drain. Serve hot. Makes 6 servings.

How To Make Chicken Kiev

Mix softened butter with seasonings. Form into 3-inch square and freeze.

While seasoned butter is frozen, cut into 6 equal pats—one for each piece of chicken.

Carefully fold sides and ends of chicken over butter mixture, making sure no butter is showing.

Singapore Chicken

Lemon sauce complements these golden tidbits of chicken.

2 whole chicken breasts,
   skinned and boned
1 tablespoon soy sauce
1 tablespoon sherry wine
1/2 teaspoon salt
1/4 teaspoon ground ginger
1/2 teaspoon sugar

1/2 cup flour
1/4 cup cornstarch
1/2 teaspoon baking powder
1 cup water
1 tablespoon cooking oil
Oil or shortening for frying
Lemon Sauce, see below

Lemon Sauce:

1 cup chicken broth or bouillon
2 tablespoons sherry wine
1 tablespoon soy sauce
1/4 teaspoon ground ginger
1 teaspoon honey

1 clove garlic, crushed
1/2 teaspoon grated lemon peel
1 tablespoon cornstarch
2 tablespoons lemon juice

Cut chicken into strips about 1/4-inch thick. Place chicken strips in large bowl. In small bowl, combine soy sauce, wine, salt, ginger and sugar. Pour marinade over chicken and let stand about 10 minutes. To make batter: In medium bowl, combine flour, cornstarch and baking powder. Stir in water and 1 tablespoon oil. Mix well. Drain chicken; dip strips in batter. Drop a few chicken strips at a time in hot oil or shortening in mini-fryer. Fry about 1-1/2 to 2 minutes or until golden brown. Drain. Serve hot with Lemon Sauce. Makes 4 servings.

Lemon Sauce:
In small saucepan, heat broth or bouillon, wine, soy sauce, ginger, honey, garlic and lemon peel. Dissolve cornstarch in lemon juice, stir into broth mixture. Cook over low heat, stirring constantly, until thick and translucent.

Frankfurters

The recipe that produces the most typical, American-style Corn Dog is simply called Corn Dogs. Frankfurters are dipped into thick batter. Tongs are handy for dipping and turning them in the batter. If you use plastic tongs, don't dip them into hot oil or shortening. If you use long metal tongs, you can pick up the coated corn dog with them, lower it into hot oil, and remove it when it is done.

If you like a thinner, more crispy coating with less cornmeal, you'll enjoy Crispy Corn Dogs. If a spicy flavor with a small amount of cornmeal sounds good to you, the Spicy Corn Dogs will be your choice.

To make them look authentic, insert a small wooden skewer in the end of each cooked corn dog. This is a perfect dish to serve at a teen-age get-together or a main dish for a youngster's birthday celebration. Add a few fresh-vegetable relishes, deviled eggs and perhaps some potato chips. Top it off with glasses of lemonade plus a slice of cake. Serve Corn Dogs on the porch or in your backyard on a hot summer evening.

For mini-fryers that are not wide enough to cook a whole Corn Dog, cut it in half before dipping it into the batter. Then serve twice as many smaller ones.

Spicy Corn Dogs

Spicy coating with slight cornmeal flavor.

1 cup biscuit mix
2 tablespoons yellow cornmeal
1/2 teaspoon dry mustard
1/4 teaspoon paprika
1/8 teaspoon cayenne pepper

1/4 teaspoon seasoned salt
1 egg
1/3 cup milk
10 frankfurters
Oil or shortening for frying

In medium bowl, stir biscuit mix with cornmeal, dry mustard, paprika, cayenne pepper, seasoned salt, egg and milk until smooth. Pat frankfurters dry with paper towels. Dip frankfurters into batter; let excess batter drip into bowl. Fry in hot oil or shortening in mini-fryer until golden brown. Drain. Serve hot. Makes 10 corn dogs.

Cheese Crumb Franks

Try these extra-crunchy cheese-coated hot dogs.

10 frankfurters
1/3 cup flour
1/2 teaspoon dry mustard
1/4 teaspoon paprika

1 egg
1 tablespoon water
1 cup finely crushed cheese-cracker crumbs
Oil or shortening for frying

Pat frankfurters dry with paper towels. In shallow dish, combine flour, dry mustard and paprika. In another shallow dish, beat egg with water, and in a third dish place cracker crumbs. Dip frankfurters in flour mixture, then in egg mixture, then in crumbs. Dip again in egg mixture, then in crumbs. Fry in hot oil or shortening in mini-fryer for 1 to 2 minutes, until golden brown and crisp. Drain. Serve hot. Makes 10 coated franks.

Crispy Corn Dogs

Wooden skewers make these neater to eat!

10 frankfurters
1 cup flour
1-1/2 teaspoons baking powder
1/2 teaspoon salt
2 tablespoons yellow cornmeal

3 tablespoons shortening
1 egg, beaten
3/4 cup milk
Oil or shortening for frying

Pat frankfurters dry with paper towels. In medium bowl, combine flour, baking powder, salt and cornmeal. Cut in shortening thoroughly. Stir in egg and milk. Dip frankfurters in batter, allowing excess batter to drip into bowl. Fry in hot oil or shortening in mini-fryer until golden brown, about 2 minutes. Insert wooden skewer in end of each corn dog, if desired. Makes 10 crispy corn dogs.

Beefy Hot Dogs

Hamburger and hot dogs—prepared as a pair!

1 lb. lean ground beef
3/4 cup soft bread crumbs
1/4 cup milk
2 tablespoons finely chopped onion
1 egg, slightly beaten
1/2 teaspoon salt

Dash pepper
6 frankfurters
Oil or shortening for frying
6 hot dog buns
Catsup Sauce, see below

Catsup Sauce:
1 cup catsup
1/4 cup butter or margarine

1/4 cup molasses
2 tablespoons vinegar

Combine ground beef with bread crumbs, milk, onion, egg, salt and pepper. Mix lightly and divide into 6 portions. Shape beef mixture around frankfurters to cover completely. Cover and chill at least 1 hour. Fry chilled frankfurters in hot oil or shortening in mini-fryer for 2 minutes. Turn and fry another 2 minutes. Drop in warm Catsup Sauce to coat. Serve on toasted buns. Makes 6 beefy hot dogs.

Catsup Sauce:
Combine catsup, butter or margarine, molasses and vinegar in small saucepan. Simmer about 5 minutes.

Corn Dogs

Special summer fun served on skewers.

1 cup flour
2/3 cups cornmeal
2 tablespoons sugar
1-1/2 teaspoons baking powder
1 teaspoon salt
2 tablespoons shortening

1 egg, beaten
3/4 cup milk
10 frankfurters
Oil or shortening for frying
Mustard and relish, if desired

In medium bowl, mix flour, cornmeal, sugar, baking powder and salt. With pastry blender or fork, cut in 2 tablespoons shortening until mixture resembles fine crumbs. In small bowl, combine egg and milk. Add to dry mixture; mix well. Pat frankfurters dry with paper towels. Dip frankfurters in batter, being careful to coat all sides. Drop 1 or 2 at a time into hot oil or shortening in mini-fryer. Fry until golden, about 1 minute on each side. Insert wooden skewer in end of each. Serve hot. Good plain or with mustard and relish, if desired. Makes 10 corn dogs.

How to Make Corn Dogs

With pastry blender or fork, cut shortening into flour mixture; then add egg and milk.

Dip frankfurters into batter with tongs; let excess batter drip off before frying.

Hot Dog Puffs

Like bite-size corn dogs!

1 egg
1/2 cup milk
1 teaspoon prepared mustard
1 cup flour
1 teaspoon baking powder

1/2 teaspoon salt
5 frankfurters
Oil or shortening for frying
Relish, catsup or mustard, if desired

In medium bowl, mix egg with milk and mustard. Stir in flour, baking powder and salt. Mix until smooth. Cut each frankfurter in 8 to 10 slices. Add to batter. Drop by tablespoons into hot oil or shortening in mini-fryer. Fry about 2-1/2 to 3 minutes, until golden brown. Drain. Serve hot with relish, catsup or additional mustard, if desired. Makes 10 puffs.

Chimichanga Hot Dogs

Mexican-food fans will love this with salsa or taco sauce.

4 flour tortillas,
  7- to 7-1/2-in. diameter
4 tablespoons refried beans
4 thin slices Monterey Jack
  or Cheddar cheese

4 frankfurters
2 teaspoons finely chopped onion
Oil or shortening for frying

Wrap tortillas in foil and warm in 275°F (135°C) oven for 5 minutes to soften. Spread 1 tablespoon refried beans in center of each warm tortilla. Top with slice of Monterey Jack or Cheddar cheese, then frankfurter. Sprinkle with onion. Carefully fold in both sides of tortilla, covering ends of frankfurter. Then fold bottom of tortilla up and over frankfurter and roll up. Insert toothpick in top to hold together. Carefully drop into hot oil or shortening in mini-fryer. Fry about 2 minutes or until golden and crisp. Drain. Serve hot. Makes 4 chimichangas.

Main Dishes

A fried entree is a savory answer to the eternal question of what to serve. The variety is practically unlimited, ranging from croquettes to sandwiches to spareribs.

Croquettes are impressive to serve, and also budget-stretchers. Next time you have leftover turkey, ham or chicken, consider grinding or chopping it and using it in one of these croquette recipes. Be aware that croquettes do take preparation time. Usually the sauce and meat should be refrigerated before being shaped. If the mixture is cool, it's easier to shape and can be coated more efficiently Don't skimp on the coating for croquettes. If the recipe calls for a coating of flour, then egg, and then crumbs, follow each step carefully. Finally chill the coated croquettes if suggested in the recipe. That second chilling process "sets" the coating and provides a shield around the meat and sauce. The result is a beautiful golden-brown crust with a moist, flavorful center. Although you may be used to croquettes in the familar cone shape,

small rectangles or log shapes fit nicely in the mini-fryers.

Thick French Toast is one of my favorite brunch or luncheon main dishes. It seems so light and puffy when made with thick egg bread. Ordinarily, it is necessary to buy unsliced bread at a bakery, then slice it yourself. If it is not convenient for you to find this kind of unsliced bread, you can use regular bread that is available in any market.

Fried Cheese Sandwiches are delicious. First, make a sandwich of mozzarella cheese, with or without thin slices of pastrami or pepperoni. This is coated with milk and crumbs to give a crunchy exterior; then dipped into an egg mixture and fried.

Perhaps you didn't realize that many sparerib dishes that are so popular in Chinese restaurants are fried. Simmer them first to make them more tender. Drain them thoroughly; fry until brown and crispy. Fried Glazed Spareribs have a glaze with a snappy flavor. Sweet-Sour Ribs are served with a more traditional Oriental Sweet-Sour Sauce.

Ham-and-Scrambled-Egg Croquettes

What a novel idea for brunch!

2 tablespoons butter or margarine
2 tablespoons flour
1/2 cup chicken broth
1-1/2 cups finely chopped cooked ham
2 tablespoons butter or margarine

4 eggs, slightly beaten
1 tablespoon minced parsley
1/4 teaspoon salt
1/2 cup flour
Oil or shortening for frying

In small saucepan, melt 2 tablespoons butter or margarine. Add 2 tablespoons flour and cook over low heat, stirring several minutes. Stir in broth and simmer 2 to 3 minutes. In a skillet, heat ham in 2 tablespoons butter or margarine. Add eggs, parsley and salt. Scramble eggs until they form soft curds. Stir egg mixture into thickened chicken broth. Butter 9" x 5" loaf dish and spread mixture evenly. Cover and chill about 2 hours or until firm. Cut into 1" x 2" rectangles. Roll in 1/2 cup flour. Carefully drop into hot oil or shortening in mini-fryer. Fry about 1-1/2 to 2 minutes until golden brown. Drain. Serve hot. Makes 18 to 20 mini-croquettes.

Fried Cheese Sandwiches

This hearty Italian sandwich makes a meal!

8 slices Italian or French bread
4 oz. mozzarella cheese
1/2 cup milk
1/2 cup fine dry seasoned bread crumbs
2 eggs

2 tablespoons milk
Oil or shortening for frying
Marinated artichoke hearts or tomatoes,
  if desired

With cookie cutter, cut slices of bread into 3-inch rounds. Slice cheese 1/4-inch thick. Make sandwiches of bread rounds and cheese. In piepan briefly dip both sides of each sandwich in 1/2 cup milk. Gently press edges together, then dip both sides in bread crumbs. To seal more securely, roll edges of sandwiches around slowly through bread crumbs. In shallow dish, dip in eggs mixed with 2 tablespoons milk. Fry in hot oil or shortening in mini-fryer about 2 minutes until brown on each side. Drain. Serve hot. Serve with marinated artichoke hearts or tomatoes, if desired. Makes 4 sandwiches.

Variation:
Add several thin slices of cooked pastrami or pepperoni to cheese in each sandwich.

Scotch Eggs

You'll find a hard-cooked egg surprise in the middle.

6 eggs
1 lb. pork sausage
1/4 cup soft bread crumbs
2 tablespoons finely chopped parsley

1/4 cup finely chopped onion
1/2 teaspoon dried tarragon
1/3 cup flour
Oil or shortening for frying

In small saucepan, boil eggs until hard-cooked, about 10 minutes. Peel, pat dry and set aside. In medium bowl, mix sausage with bread crumbs, parsley, onion and tarragon. Completely cover each egg with sausage mixture. Roll in flour. Fry in hot oil or shortening in mini-fryer about 4 to 5 minutes until brown on all sides and sausage is done. Sausage may crack occasionally while frying. Serve warm or cool. Cut in wedges for appetizers, or serve halves on luncheon plate, or tuck a whole Scotch Egg in the lunch box or picnic basket. Makes 6 coated eggs.

French Toast

A classic favorite for breakfast, lunch or Sunday brunch.

2 eggs
1/3 cup milk
1/4 teaspoon salt
4 (1-in.-thick) slices bread

Oil or shortening for frying
Maple syrup, honey or fruit-flavored syrup
Sausage links or sliced ham, if desired

In shallow dish, beat eggs with milk and salt. Trim crusts from bread, cut slices in half if necessary to fit mini-fryer. Dip into egg mixture. Let stand a few seconds. Turn bread and repeat for other side. With slotted spoon or mini-basket, carefully lower bread into hot oil or shortening in mini-fryer. Fry about 2 minutes, until golden brown. Drain. Serve hot with maple syrup, honey, or fruit-flavored syrup. Good with sausage links or sliced ham. Makes 4 slices French toast.

Beef & Potato Meatballs

Meat 'n potatoes together make delicious mini-meatballs.

1 lb. lean ground beef
1 (12-oz.) pkg. frozen hash-brown
  potatoes, thawed
1/2 cup finely chopped onions
1 egg
1 teaspoon curry powder

1 teaspoon salt
1/4 teaspoon pepper
Oil or shortening for frying
Sweet-Sour Sauce, page 53, if desired
Cream-of-mushroom soup, if desired

In medium bowl, mix together beef, potatoes, onions, egg, curry, salt and pepper. Form into 1-inch balls. Fry in hot oil or shortening in mini-fryer about 4 minutes until done inside. Drain. Serve hot. Serve plain or with Sweet-Sour Sauce, page 53, or with undiluted cream-of-mushroom soup, if desired. Makes 50 mini-meatballs.

Egg Croquettes

Bite into these crusty croquettes, with a soft egg mixture inside.

2 tablespoons butter or margarine
2 tablespoons flour
1/2 cup milk
4 hard-cooked eggs, finely chopped
1 tablespoon grated onion
2 tablespoons finely chopped parsley
1/2 teaspoon dry mustard

1/2 teaspoon celery salt
1/8 teaspoon pepper
1/2 cup flour
1 egg, slightly beaten
1-1/2 cups soft bread crumbs
Oil or shortening for frying

In heavy saucepan, melt butter or margarine. Stir in 2 tablespoons flour. Pour in milk, stirring constantly. Bring to boil. Stir and simmer several minutes. Remove from heat. Add hard-cooked eggs, onion, parsley, dry mustard, celery salt and pepper. Refrigerate mixture several hours or until thoroughly chilled. Divide mixture in 6 equal parts. Shape each in a cylinder about 3 inches long and 1 inch in diameter. In a shallow dish, dip croquettes in 1/2 cup flour. In a small bowl, dip in egg, then roll in bread crumbs in piepan. Refrigerate another 20 to 30 minutes. Fry in hot oil or shortening in mini-fryer until golden. Drain. Serve hot. Makes 6 croquettes.

Stir together sauce, cooked eggs and seasonings; then refrigerate several hours.

How To Make
Egg Croquettes

Divide chilled mixture into 6 parts; shape each part into cylinder or "log" about 3" x 1."

Roll chilled croquettes in flour, then in egg, then in bread crumbs. Chill again before frying.

Pizza Balls

Here's a meatball for all pizza fans.

1 egg
1 cup soft bread crumbs
1/2 cup milk
1/2 teaspoon garlic salt
1/8 teaspoon pepper
2 tablespoons instant minced onion
1/2 teaspoon oregano

1 lb. lean ground beef
1-1/2 to 2 oz. Monterey Jack cheese,
    cut in 1/2-in. cubes
1/4 cup flour
Oil or shortening for frying
1 (8- to 10-oz.) can pizza sauce

In medium bowl, beat egg. Stir in bread crumbs, milk, garlic salt, pepper, onion and oregano. Mix in beef. Shape a rounded tablespoon of meat mixture into ball, placing a cheese cube in the center. Coat with flour. Fry in hot oil or shortening in mini-fryer 3 minutes until brown. Drain. In small saucepan, heat pizza sauce. Serve over hot fried meatballs. Makes 20 to 25 balls.

Turkey-and-Ham Croquettes

A great way to glamorize leftovers.

1/4 cup butter or margarine
1/4 cup flour
1/2 cup chicken broth
1/2 cup milk
1 cup minced cooked turkey or chicken
1/2 cup boiled or baked ham, finely chopped
1 teaspoon minced parsley

1/8 teaspoon nutmeg
1/2 teaspoon seasoned salt
1/2 cup flour
1 egg, slightly beaten
1/4 cup seasoned bread crumbs
Oil or shortening for frying

In saucepan, melt butter or margarine. Add 1/4 cup flour and cook over low heat, stirring for several minutes. Stir in broth and milk. Simmer for another 2 to 3 minutes. Remove from heat. Add turkey or chicken, ham, parsley, nutmeg and seasoned salt. Butter 9" x 5" loaf dish, and spread mixture evenly. Cover and chill about 2 hours until fairly firm. Cut in rectangles about 1" x 2." In shallow dish, coat rectangles with 1/2 cup flour. In small bowl, dip in egg; then in a piepan, roll in bread crumbs. Carefully drop into hot oil or shortening in mini-fryer. Fry about 1-1/2 to 2 minutes or until golden brown. Drain. Serve hot. Makes 16 croquettes.

Chimichangas

A Mexican favorite similar to burritos, but fried until crisp and golden.

9 large flour tortillas (8-in. diameter)
Oil or shortening for frying
1 (6-oz.) can frozen guacamole dip, thawed
1 cup sour cream

1 (7-oz.) can green chili salsa
1 small onion, chopped
1 medium tomato, chopped
Beef or Pork Filling, see below

Beef Filling:
1/2 lb. lean ground beef
1 small onion, chopped
1 small green pepper, chopped
1 clove garlic, minced
1/4 teaspoon salt

1/4 teaspoon ground cumin
1 tablespoon chili powder
1/8 teaspoon cayenne pepper
1/3 cup canned refried beans
3/4 cup shredded Monterey Jack cheese

Pork Filling:
1 lb. lean boneless pork
1 tablespoon cooking oil
1 small onion, chopped
1 clove garlic, minced
1/2 teaspoon salt

1/4 teaspoon oregano leaves
2 tablespoons chopped fresh cilantro leaves
1/2 cup diced green chiles
1 tablespoon water

Make either Beef or Pork Filling and set aside. Place 1/4 cup of either Beef or Pork Filling in center of each tortilla. Fold bottom, then fold both sides over filling and roll up. If tortillas are hard to roll, sprinkle lightly with water and wrap in foil. Heat in 350°F (177°C) oven for 5 to 8 minutes, or until warm and pliable. Secure rolled tortillas with toothpick. Carefully drop Chimichangas into hot oil or shortening in mini-fryer. Fry 1 to 2 minutes, or until golden and crispy. Drain and serve hot. Top each Chimichanga with about 1-1/2 tablespoons guacamole dip and about 1 tablespoon sour cream. Serve with a bowl of green chili salsa mixed with onion and tomatoes. Makes enough for 9 Chimichangas.

Beef Filling:
In skillet, brown ground beef. Stir with fork to break up meat. Add onion, green pepper and garlic. Cook, stirring until onion is soft. Stir in salt, cumin, chili powder, cayenne pepper and beans. Cook, stirring constantly, over medium heat until hot. Remove from heat; stir in cheese and set aside to cool.

Pork Filling:
After trimming off fat, cut pork in 1/2-inch cubes. Heat 1 tablespoon oil in skillet over medium-high heat. Add pork to cook until lightly browned. Add onion and garlic, cook until onion is soft. Stir in salt, oregano, cilantro, chiles and water. Cover and cook over low heat, stirring occasionally, for 35 to 45 minutes or until pork is very tender. Remove cover of pan the last few minutes of cooking to evaporate liquid. Set aside to cool.

Salmon Balls

Mini-croquettes for a main dish.

1 medium potato, peeled
1 medium onion, peeled
1 (1-lb.) can salmon, drained and flaked
1-1/2 tablespoons flour
1 egg, slightly beaten

1/2 teaspoon salt
1/8 teaspoon pepper
1/2 cup fine dry bread crumbs
Oil or shortening for frying
1 (10-oz.) pkg. frozen creamed peas

In medium bowl, coarsely grate potato and onion. Add salmon, flour, egg, salt and pepper. Mix well. Shape into 20 to 24 balls about 1 inch in diameter. In shallow dish, roll balls in bread crumbs. Refrigerate at least 1 hour. Drop into hot oil or shortening in mini-fryer. Fry about 2 minutes or until brown. Drain. Serve hot. Prepare creamed peas according to package directions. Serve over Salmon Balls. Makes 4 to 5 servings.

Chicken-Almond Croquettes

Next time try ham instead of chicken.

3 tablespoons butter or margarine
3 tablespoons flour
1 cup milk
1/4 teaspoon salt
1/4 teaspoon garlic salt
1/2 teaspoon chili powder
1/2 cup chopped almonds

2-1/2 cups finely ground cooked chicken
 or turkey
1 tablespoon lemon juice
3/4 cup fine dry bread crumbs
1 egg
1 tablespoon water
Oil or shortening for frying

In a saucepan, melt butter or margarine over moderate heat. Stir in flour. Slowly stir in milk. Add salt, garlic salt, and chili powder. Cook, stirring until thick. Remove from heat. Add almonds, chicken or turkey and lemon juice. Spread mixture on a platter to cool. Shape into 12 logs. Roll in bread crumbs. Let stand about 5 minutes. In small bowl, beat egg with water. Dip each croquette in egg mixture. Roll again in crumbs. Refrigerate croquettes 30 minutes. Fry in hot oil or shortening in mini-fryer 2 to 2-1/2 minutes. Turn and fry another 2 minutes. Drain. Serve hot. Makes 12 croquettes.

Breaded Veal Cutlets

Perfect for your most discriminating guests.

1/3 cup flour
1 teaspoon salt
1/4 teaspoon pepper
3/4 lb. thin veal cutlets
1 egg, slightly beaten

1/2 cup fine dry bread crumbs
Oil or shortening for frying
Lemon slices, for garnish
Cream sauce, if desired

In shallow bowl or piepan, combine flour, salt and pepper. Dip veal cutlets in flour mixture. In separate shallow dishes, dip veal in egg, then in bread crumbs. Gently drop veal into hot oil or shortening in mini-fryer. Fry about 2 to 3 minutes, until golden brown and done. Drain. Serve hot with lemon slices or cream sauce, if desired. Makes 3 to 4 servings.

Sweet-Sour Ribs

Solve your menu problem with these succulent ribs.

2 lbs. spareribs
Water
2 tablespoons cornstarch
2 tablespoons soy sauce

1/2 teaspoon salt
2 tablespoons honey
Oil or shortening for frying
Sweet-Sour Sauce, see below

Sweet-Sour Sauce:
1 tablespoon cornstarch
2 tablespoons brown sugar
2 tablespoons vinegar

1 tablespoon soy sauce
1 (8-oz.) can pineapple chunks, not drained

Cut ribs into 1- or 2-rib pieces. In large pan, cover ribs with water. Bring to a boil, simmer 20 minutes. Drain thoroughly. Pat dry with paper towels. In shallow dish, combine 2 tablespoons cornstarch, 2 tablespoons soy sauce, salt and honey. Blend well. Coat drained ribs with honey mixture. Fry in hot oil or shortening in mini-fryer about 1 minute until brown and crispy. Drain. Spoon Sweet-Sour Sauce over fried ribs and serve warm. Makes 3 to 4 servings.

Sweet-Sour Sauce:
While ribs are cooking, combine cornstarch and brown sugar in saucepan, stir in vinegar and soy sauce. Add pineapple chunks with juice. Cook, stirring constantly, until sauce is thick and translucent.

Tuna Croquettes

When you taste these you'll wish you had doubled the recipe.

2 tablespoons butter or margarine
2 tablespoons finely chopped onion
2 tablespoons flour
1/8 teaspoon salt
1/2 teaspoon Worcestershire sauce

1/3 cup milk
1 (6-1/2-oz.) can tuna
1 teaspoon lemon juice
1/2 cup finely crushed corn flakes
Oil or shortening for frying

In small saucepan, melt butter or margarine. Add onion and cook until tender. Blend in flour and salt. Add Worcestershire sauce and milk. Cook over low heat, stirring constantly, until thick. Drain and flake tuna. Stir tuna and lemon juice into sauce mixture. Refrigerate until thoroughly chilled. Form into small log-like croquettes about 1" x 2." Roll in crushed corn flakes. Carefully drop into hot oil or shortening in mini-fryer. Fry about 1 minute until crisp and golden. Makes 10 croquettes.

Fried Glazed Spareribs

Spareribs with a new look and great taste.

2 lbs. spareribs
Water
1 tablespoon soy sauce
1 egg, slightly beaten

1/4 cup flour
Oil or shortening for frying
Soy-Onion Glaze, see below

Soy-Onion Glaze:
1/2 cup sugar
1/2 cup wine vinegar

1/4 cup soy sauce
2 tablespoons sliced green onions

Cut spareribs into 1- or 2-rib pieces. Place ribs in large pan and cover with water. Bring to boil. Simmer 20 minutes. Drain thoroughly. Pat dry with paper towels. In shallow dish, combine 1 tablespoon soy sauce, egg and flour. Brush spareribs with egg mixture. Fry in hot oil or shortening in mini-fryer about 2 to 3 minutes, until brown and crispy. Drain. Brush hot fried spareribs with Soy-Onion Glaze. Makes 3 to 4 servings.

Soy-Onion Glaze:
In saucepan, heat sugar, wine vinegar, 1/4 cup soy sauce and green onions. Cook over medium heat, stirring constantly, until mixture is syrupy.

Turkey-Carrot Croquettes

What a way to dress up leftover turkey!

2 cups finely chopped, cooked turkey
    or chicken
2 eggs, slightly beaten
1 (10-1/2-oz.) can cream-of-chicken soup,
    undiluted
1 tablespoon Worcestershire sauce

1/4 cup finely chopped onion
1 medium carrot, peeled and grated
1 cup fine dry bread crumbs
1/2 cup fine cracker crumbs
Oil or shortening for frying
Cream sauce, if desired

In medium bowl, combine turkey or chicken, eggs, soup, Worcestershire sauce, onion, carrot and bread crumbs. Mix well. Cover and chill several hours. Shape into small logs about 1" x 2." In pie-pan, roll logs in cracker crumbs. Carefully drop into hot oil or shortening in mini-fryer. Fry about 2 to 2-1/2 minutes until golden brown. Drain. Serve hot. Good plain or with cream sauce, if desired. Makes about 25 croquettes.

Spring Rolls

Or do you call them egg rolls?

1/2 lb. uncooked shrimp, in shell
1/2 cup uncooked lean pork
2 tablespoons cooking oil
1/2 cup chopped celery
1/2 cup fresh or canned bean sprouts
4 medium mushrooms, chopped
1 tablespoon soy sauce
1 tablespoon sherry wine

1/2 teaspoon salt
1 tablespoon cornstarch
2 tablespoons water
12 to 16 egg roll skins
Oil or shortening for frying
Mustard or Quick Chinese-Plum Sauce,
    page 152, if desired

Shell and clean shrimp. Finely chop shrimp and pork. In skillet, heat 2 tablespoons oil. Add shrimp, pork and celery. Stir-fry for several minutes, then add bean sprouts, mushrooms, soy sauce, wine and salt. Heat to boiling. Dissolve cornstarch in 2 tablespoons water. Add to meat mixture. Cook over low heat, stirring constantly, until thick and translucent. Place about 2 tablespoons mixture diagonally across bottom of each egg roll skin. Fold bottom corner up over filling. Fold side corners in toward center. Roll up, brush water on edges and press to seal. Drop 1 or 2 at a time in hot oil or shortening in mini-fryer. Fry 1-1/2 to 2 minutes until golden and crisp. Serve plain, or with mustard or Quick Chinese-Plum Sauce, page 152, if desired. Cut into 1-inch slices for appetizers or leave whole for entree. Makes 12 to 16 rolls.

Note:
Egg roll skins or wrappers are available in Oriental markets, gourmet shops and the frozen-food or deli sections of many supermarkets.

Empanadas (Mexican Turnovers)

Terrific warm, or as a picnic or lunch box special.

1 cup flour
1 teaspoon baking powder
1/2 teaspoon salt
1/4 cup shortening

2 to 3 tablespoons ice water
Oil or shortening for frying
Spicy Beef Filling, see below

Spicy Beef Filling:
2 tablespoons chopped onion
1/2 lb. lean ground beef
1 tablespoon cooking oil
1 small tomato, chopped
1/4 teaspoon cinnamon

1/2 teaspoon salt
1/4 teaspoon chili powder
2 tablespoons chopped raisins
1/4 cup chopped blanched almonds

Prepare Spicy Beef Filling and set aside. In medium bowl, combine flour, baking powder, and salt. Cut in 1/4 cup shortening with pastry blender or fork until mixture resembles crumbs. Gradually add enough ice water to hold dough together. Divide dough into 6 portions. Roll out each into a 5-inch pastry circle. Place about 2 tablespoons Spicy Beef Filling on half of each circle. Brush edges with water. Fold in half, pressing edges firmly to seal in filling. Fry in hot oil or shortening in mini-fryer, 2 to 3 minutes until golden. Drain. Serve warm or cool. Makes 6 turnovers.

Spicy Beef Filling:
In skillet, saute onion and beef in 1 tablespoon oil. Drain excess oil. Stir in tomato, cinnamon, salt, chili powder, raisins and almonds. Cover and simmer 5 minutes. Cool slightly.

Potatoes

In the U.S.A. there is perhaps nothing more synonymous with deep-frying than French-fried potatoes. It is rare to see a hot dog or hamburger ordered in a fast-food establishment without French fries. Your mini-fryer makes excellent French fries—use it often to satisfy that French-fry craving. Potatoes prepared in a variety of ways are excellent when deep-fried, so don't miss out on the other distinctive tastes—try all the recipes in this section.

Let's talk first about "fries" and "chips." It is almost universally accepted that a really good French fry must first be soaked in water to remove starch, and be fried *twice*. If you are in a hurry, you can get by with frying them only once with satisfactory results. However, the second frying gives you superior quality. The results are more crisp and better tasting, with less shriveling.

For potato chips, the real secret is a very thin potato slice. You can do this with a very sharp knife, but I prefer to use a vegetable peeler.

The frying times given in the following recipes should be about right for the thickness of potatoes specified. However, frying time will vary with the thickness of the piece, moisture content and the quantity in the mini-fryer. Consequently you may have to experiment a bit at first. You'll quickly find correct timing for your particular cut of fries or chips. Just remember that the degree of doneness is in direct relation to the degree of bubbling. For instance; chips stop bubbling when done and fries bubble very lazily when done.

In frying uncoated potatoes, it is difficult to remove all moisture by patting them with paper towels. Consequently, very active bubbling and some splattering will occur when the potatoes are lowered into hot oil or shortening. If your mini-fryer came with a fryer basket, use it. Slowly lower uncoated potatoes into hot oil or shortening. If excessive bubbling and splattering occurs, lift the basket out of the oil momentarily; then lower into the oil again. If you don't have a fryer basket, use a slotted spoon in the same manner. That is, don't drop the potatoes off the spoon into the oil until you are sure excessive bubbling and splattering will not be a problem. It's a good idea to separate the potato pieces with a slotted spoon immediately after dropping them into hot oil.

Frozen French Fries

It's hard to beat frozen French fries for convenience, crispness and eye appeal.

1 lb. frozen French-fried potatoes
Oil or shortening for frying

Salt to taste

Carefully lower 10 to 14 frozen fries into hot oil or shortening in mini-fryer. Fry 4 to 5 minutes or until golden and done inside. Drain. Sprinkle with salt to taste. Serve hot. Makes 5 to 6 servings.

Variation:
Sprinkle with seasoned salt for a different flavor.

Natural French Fries

Unpeeled potatoes give more natural flavor to these French fries.

2 medium potatoes
Water
Oil or shortening for frying

Seasoned salt to taste
Grated Parmesan cheese to taste

Wash potatoes thoroughly. Pat dry. Cut each into 8 wedges. In medium bowl, soak in cold water for 30 minutes; change water once. Drain. Pat dry with paper towels. Pre-fry 8 or 9 slices in hot oil or shortening in mini-fryer for 2 minutes. Drain. Cool at least 10 minutes. Just before serving, fry again in hot oil or shortening for 8 to 9 minutes until brown and done inside. Drain. Sprinkle with seasoned salt and grated Parmesan cheese to taste. Serve hot. Makes 3 to 4 servings.

Food-Processor French Fries

These soft-centered potato slices complement any entree.

2 medium potatoes
Water

Oil or shortening for frying
Salt to taste

Peel potatoes and shape to fit processor's feed tube; feed through slicer. In medium bowl, soak slices in cold water about 30 minutes, changing water once. Drain. Pat dry with paper towels. Fry 8 to 10 slices at a time in hot oil or shortening in mini-fryer 3-1/2 to 4 minutes, or until golden brown. Drain. Sprinkle with salt to taste, and serve hot. Makes 3 to 4 servings.

Kitchen French Fries

Larger fries make English-style "Fish 'n Chips."

2 medium potatoes
Water

Oil or shortening for frying
Salt to taste

Peel potatoes. Cut in 1/4- to 1/2-inch-thick strips. In medium bowl, soak in cold water for 30 minutes, changing water once. Drain. Pat dry with paper towels. Fry 8 to 10 at a time in hot oil or shortening in mini-fryer 6 to 8 minutes or until brown and done inside. Drain. Sprinkle with salt to taste. Serve hot. Makes 3 to 4 servings.

Variation:
For English-style "Fish 'n Chips," cut potatoes into larger strips, 5/8- to 3/4-inch thick, and fry 8 to 10 minutes.

Traditional French Fries

Good basic French fries!

2 medium potatoes
Water

Oil or shortening for frying
Salt to taste

Peel potatoes. Cut in 1/4- to 1/2-inch-thick strips. In medium bowl, soak potato strips in cold water for 30 minutes, changing water once. Drain. Pat dry with paper towels. Pre-fry 8 to 10 strips at a time in hot oil or shortening in mini-fryer 1-1/2 to 2 minutes. Drain; let stand to cool at least 10 minutes. Just before serving, fry again in hot oil or shortening 5 to 6 minutes or until golden brown and done inside. Drain. Sprinkle with salt to taste and serve hot. Makes 3 to 4 servings.

Hash-Brown Haystacks

They resemble hash browns—but taste even better.

1 small onion
3 large potatoes
2 eggs, separated

1/2 teaspoon salt
Oil or shortening for frying
Applesauce or sour cream, if desired

Peel, grate and drain onion and potatoes. In small bowl, beat egg whites until stiff and dry. In medium bowl, combine well-drained onions and potatoes, slightly beaten egg yolks and salt. Fold in beaten egg whites. Immediately drop by tablespoons into hot oil or shortening in mini-fryer. Fry until golden brown, about 2 to 3 minutes. Drain. Serve plain, or topped with applesauce or sour cream, if desired. Makes about 3 to 4 servings.

Traditional French Fries

Delta French Fries

A cheesy twist to the ever-popular French fries.

2 large potatoes
Water
1 egg
1 tablespoon water

3/4 cup (about 16) finely crushed
    cheese crackers
Oil or shortening for frying
Salt to taste

Peel potatoes and cut in sticks like French fries. In medium bowl, soak sticks in cold water for 30 minutes; change water once. In small bowl, beat egg slightly with water. Drain potatoes and pat dry with paper towels. Dip potatoes into egg mixture, then in another small bowl, dip potatoes in crumbs. Fry in hot oil or shortening in mini-fryer about 1 minute or until brown. Drain. Sprinkle with salt to taste. Serve hot. Makes 3 to 4 servings.

Pre-Baked French Fries

Oven-baked potatoes provide a more flavorful French fry.

2 medium potatoes
Water

Oil or shortening for frying
Salt to taste

Peel potatoes. Cut in 1/4- to 1/2-inch-thick strips. In medium bowl, soak in cold water for 30 minutes, changing water once. Drain. Pat dry with paper towels. Arrange potato strips in single layer on wire rack in broiler pan. Bake in 250°F (121°C) oven about 20 minutes. Pre-fry 8 to 10 strips at a time in hot oil or shortening in mini-fryer for 1-1/2 to 2 minutes. Drain. Let stand to cool at least 10 minutes. Just before serving, fry again in hot oil or shortening for 5 to 6 minutes or until golden and done inside. Drain. Sprinkle with salt. Serve hot. Makes 3 to 4 servings.

Matchstick Potatoes

Mini-version of standard French fries.

2 medium potatoes
Water

Oil or shortening for frying
Salt to taste

Peel potatoes. Cut into slices about 1/8-inch thick. Then cut each slice into very thin sticks, about the size of a kitchen match. In medium bowl, cover with cold water and let stand a few minutes. Drain thoroughly. Pat dry with paper towels. Drop a few at a time into hot oil or shortening in mini-fryer. Fry until golden brown or about 1-1/2 to 2 minutes. Drain. Sprinkle with salt to taste and serve hot. Makes 2 to 3 servings.

Potato Nests

Get bird's nest baskets from your gourmet shop for this specialty.

2 medium potatoes, peeled
Water
Oil or shortening for frying

Salt to taste
Creamed vegetable, chicken, eggs or
   fish, if desired

Coarsely grate potatoes. In medium bowl, drop into cold water for 5 to 10 minutes. Squeeze out moisture and pat dry with paper towels. Dip bird's nest baskets into hot oil or shortening in mini-fryer to prevent sticking. Line the larger basket with about 1/2-inch layer of potatoes. Clamp on smaller basket. Fry in hot oil or shortening in mini-fryer for 2 to 3 minutes, or until crisp and golden. Drain. Let cool 2 to 3 minutes. Remove clamps and lift out smaller basket. Carefully un-mold fried nest. Sprinkle with salt to taste. Fill with creamed vegetable, chicken, eggs or fish, if desired. Makes 6 to 8 nests, depending on size of potatoes.

Note:
Bird's nest baskets are available in gourmet shops and in the housewares section of some department stores. Diameter of the larger basket should not exceed 4 inches for most mini-fryers.

Mini Potato Puffs

A mini-potato with a maxi appeal!

1/2 cup water
1/2 cup milk
2 tablespoons butter or margarine
1/2 teaspoon salt

1-1/3 cups dry instant mashed potatoes
2 eggs, slightly beaten
Oil or shortening for frying

In saucepan, heat water, milk, butter or margarine and salt to boiling. Remove from heat, stir in dry instant potatoes. Cool about 10 minutes. Stir eggs into potato mixture. Refrigerate until cold, about 2 hours. Shape into 18 to 20 (1-1/2-inch) balls. Drop into hot oil or shortening in mini-fryer. Fry until golden brown, about 1 to 2 minutes. Makes 18 to 20 puffs.

Potato Puffs

Take time for these!

1-1/2 lbs. potatoes
Water
1/4 cup dairy sour cream
1 egg, slightly beaten
2 tablespoons chopped chives
1 tablespoon melted butter

1/2 teaspoon salt
1/2 cup flour
1/2 cup milk
1 egg, slightly beaten
1/2 cup fine dry bread crumbs
Oil or shortening for frying

Peel potatoes and cut in quarters. In saucepan, cover potatoes with water and boil until tender. Drain thoroughly. Put through ricer or sieve. Add sour cream, 1 egg, chives, butter and salt. Stir to blend well. Chill for 1 hour. With lightly floured hands, form into balls about 1-1/2 inches in diameter. In small bowl, coat with flour. Chill another 2 hours. In small bowl, combine milk and 1 egg. Dip chilled potato balls in milk-egg mixture, then in another bowl dip balls in bread crumbs. Drop into hot oil or shortening in mini-fryer. Fry 3 or 4 at a time until golden, about 1 minute. Drain. Bake in 400°F (204°C) oven for 4 minutes or until they puff slightly and crack. Makes 25 to 30 puffs.

Potato Balls

Superb taste compensates for the time you spend.

4 medium potatoes, peeled,
  cooked and mashed
2 tablespoons butter or margarine
1/2 cup grated Cheddar cheese
1/2 teaspoon salt
2 tablespoons light cream
2 egg yolks, slightly beaten

1/2 teaspoon baking powder
1/2 cup flour
1 whole egg
2 tablespoons water
3/4 cup fine dry bread crumbs
Oil or shortening for frying

In medium bowl, combine mashed potatoes with butter or margarine, grated Cheddar cheese, salt, cream, egg yolks and baking powder. Shape into 1-1/2-inch balls. In shallow dishes, roll balls in flour, then dip in egg slightly beaten with water, and dip balls in bread crumbs. Refrigerate 1 hour. Drop into hot oil or shortening in mini-fryer. Cook until brown, about 1 to 1-1/2 minutes. Drain. Serve hot. Makes 22 to 25 balls.

How To Make Potato Balls

Bake potatoes until tender, peel and mash. Add cheese, egg yolks and other ingredients to form balls.

Before frying, roll potato balls in flour, whole-egg mixture and bread crumbs; then refrigerate.

Potato Clouds

Rain or shine, you can count on these to please!

1/2 cup flour
1 teaspoon baking powder
1/4 teaspoon salt
1 cup cooked mashed potatoes

1 egg, slightly beaten
1 teaspoon minced chives
1 teaspoon parsley
Oil or shortening for frying

In medium bowl, combine flour, baking powder, salt, mashed potatoes, egg, chives and parsley. Drop by teaspoon into hot oil or shortening in mini-fryer. Fry until golden, about 2 to 2-1/2 minutes. Drain. Serve hot. Makes 18 potato clouds.

Mock Pommes Soufflés

Crisp outside and hollow inside like the famous French potato puff.

3 medium potatoes, peeled,
  cooked and mashed
1/4 teaspoon onion salt
1/8 teaspoon pepper

1/4 teaspoon seasoned salt
1 cup flour
1/4 cup sour cream
1/2 cup flour

Mix potatoes with onion salt, pepper, seasoned salt and 1 cup flour. Stir in sour cream. Mixture should be a thick dough. Knead several times on lightly floured board. Form in 1-inch balls. Flatten with rolling pin to make a thin oval. In piepan, dip in 1/2 cup flour. Drop into hot oil or shortening in mini-fryer. Fry about 2 minutes or until golden and puffy. Drain. Serve hot. Makes 30 to 35 puffs.

Traditional Potato Chips

There is nothing quite so good as freshly fried potato chips.

2 medium potatoes
Water

Oil or shortening for frying
Salt to taste

Peel potatoes. Cut into very thin slices, less than 1/16-inch thick. Soak in cold water for 20 to 30 minutes, changing water once. Drain. Pat dry with paper towels. Fry 8 to 10 slices at a time in hot oil or shortening in mini-fryer 2 to 2-1/2 minutes or until golden brown and crisp. Drain. Sprinkle with salt to taste. Makes 60 to 80 chips, depending on size of potatoes and thickness of slices.

Note:
A vegetable peeler is ideal for slicing potatoes for chips. The slicer on a hand grater may also be used.

Pre-Salted Potato Chips

Salting before frying gives a crisper chip.

2 medium potatoes
Water

Salt
Oil or shortening for frying

Peel potatoes. Cut into very thin slices, less than 1/16-inch thick. Soak in cold water for 20 to 30 minutes, changing water once. Drain. Pat dry with paper towels. Arrange single layer of potato slices on bottom of pie plate. Sprinkle lightly with salt. Repeat layering and salting potato slices until all are arranged in plate. Cover with plastic wrap and let stand about 1 hour. Drain. Pat dry with paper towels. Fry 8 to 10 slices at a time in hot oil or shortening in mini-fryer 2 to 2-1/2 minutes or until golden brown and crisp. Drain. Serve hot. Makes 60 to 80 chips, depending on size of potatoes and thickness of slices.

Favorite Potato Chips

A super potato chip! The extra effort pays big dividends in taste and crispness.

2 medium potatoes
Water

Oil or shortening for frying
Salt to taste

Peel potatoes. Cut in very thin slices, less than 1/16-inch thick. In medium bowl, soak in cold water for 30 minutes, changing water once. Drain. Pat dry with paper towels. Arrange slices in single layer on wire rack in broiler pan. Place in 250°F (121°C) oven for 15 to 20 minutes. Fry 8 to 10 slices in hot oil or shortening in mini-fryer 2 to 2-1/2 minutes, or until crisp and golden. Drain. Sprinkle with salt to taste while hot. Makes 60 to 80 chips, depending on size of potatoes and thickness of slices.

Note:
A vegetable peeler is ideal for slicing potatoes for chips. The slicer on a hand grater may also be used.

Frozen Shredded Potato Rolls

Two minutes from freezer to table!

1 lb. frozen shredded potato rolls,
   such as Ore-Ida® Tater Tots®
Oil or shortening for frying

Salt to taste
Grated American or Parmesan cheese,
   if desired

Gently lower 10 to 14 frozen potato rolls into hot oil or shortening in mini-fryer. Fry 2 to 3 minutes or until golden brown. Drain. Sprinkle with salt to taste and serve hot. Makes 5 to 6 servings. Sprinkle with grated American or Parmesan cheese, if desired.

Vegetables

The shapes and forms of fried vegetables seem endless. You can chop, slice, grate, dice, quarter, halve, or even fry some of them whole. After you get them into one of these shapes, you can marinate them in all kinds of seasonings; then coat them with flour, egg, crumbs, cornmeal or a batter made of a combination of ingredients. In other words, the sky's the limit.

Naturally, each vegetable needs to be prepared according to it's characteristics. You'll marvel at fried zucchini. Zucchini Sticks have a coating of flour, egg and bread crumbs. You can use that same coating recipe and cut the zucchini into thin circles, long wedges, or thick chunks. Each shape will have an entirely different look, yet the flavor remains the same. If you want still another variation on the zucchini theme, try Zucchini Fritters. They are grated, mixed into a batter, and dropped

into hot oil or shortening in the mini-fryer.

When dropping food into the mini-fryer, drop it very carefully. For vegetable-fritter batters, drop by teaspoons or tablespoons, as indicated on the recipe. Hold the spoon with the uncooked fritter in it as close as possible to the hot oil or shortening. Then, with a second spoon, gently push the batter off the first spoon into the hot oil or shortening. When it is brown on one side, turn it over with a metal slotted spoon or turner. Continue cooking on the other side until golden brown or for the time suggested in the recipe. Carefully lift it out with a slotted spoon and drain on paper towels.

Most vegetables do not need to be pre-cooked before frying. Whole okra and fresh green beans are exceptions to this rule. They are more tender if simmered several minutes before being fried.

Fried Artichoke Hearts

Adds a gourmet touch to any menu.

1 (9-oz.) pkg. frozen artichoke hearts
1 egg
1 tablespoon water
3/4 cup fine dry bread crumbs
1/4 teaspoon salt

1/8 teaspoon pepper
1/4 teaspoon garlic salt
1/8 teaspoon paprika
Oil or shortening for frying
Lemon wedges, if desired

Partially thaw artichoke hearts. Pat dry with paper towels. In small bowl, beat egg with water. In shallow dish, combine crumbs with salt, pepper, garlic salt and paprika. Dip artichokes in egg mixture, then into crumbs. Fry in hot oil or shortening in mini-fryer for 2 to 3 minutes, or until brown and artichokes are done. Cooking time will vary with size of artichoke. Drain. Serve hot. Squeeze lemon over hot artichokes just before eating, if desired. Makes 3 to 4 servings.

French-Fried Asparagus

Crisp with a lacy look.

2 tablespoons flour
2 tablespoons evaporated milk, undiluted
1 egg, beaten

1 lb. asparagus
Oil or shortening for frying
Salt and pepper to taste

In small bowl, combine flour, evaporated milk and egg. Mix until smooth. Trim and wash asparagus. Drain and pat dry with paper towels. Cut each trimmed stalk in half. Dip in batter. Let excess batter drip into bowl. Fry in hot oil or shortening in mini-fryer about 1 minute or until coating is golden and crispy. Drain. Sprinkle with salt and pepper to taste. Serve hot. Makes about 6 servings.

Green-Bean Fritters

Don't be surprised if each one is a different shape.

1-1/2 cups flour
3 teaspoons baking powder
3/4 teaspoon salt
1 egg, beaten
1 cup milk

1 (16-oz.) can cut green beans,
 thoroughly drained
Oil or shortening for frying
Seasoned salt to taste

In medium bowl, combine the flour, baking powder and salt. In small bowl, combine egg, milk and beans. Add to dry ingredients. Mix just until moistened. Drop batter by tablespoons into hot oil or shortening in mini-fryer. Fry 3 to 4 minutes until golden brown, turning once. Drain. Sprinkle with seasoned salt to taste. Makes about 24 fritters.

Deviled Brussels Sprouts

Deviled Sauce gives a flavor lift to Brussels sprouts.

1 pint Brussels sprouts
1 egg, slightly beaten
1/4 cup fine dry bread crumbs

Oil or shortening for frying
Deviled Sauce, see below

Deviled Sauce:
2 tablespoons butter
1 teaspoon prepared mustard

1/2 teaspoon Worcestershire sauce
1 tablespoon catsup

Trim and wash Brussels sprouts. Pat dry with paper towels. In small bowl, dip in egg, then in shallow dish, dip Brussels sprouts in bread crumbs. Carefully drop into hot oil or shortening in mini-fryer. Fry about 1 minute on each side, or until brown and tender. Drain. Drizzle Deviled Sauce over hot Brussels sprouts. Serve hot. Makes 10 to 15, depending on size.

Deviled Sauce:
In small saucepan, melt butter. Stir in mustard, Worcestershire sauce and catsup.

Fried Carrot Nuggets

The true carrot flavor comes through with every bite.

6 medium carrots, peeled and
   cut in thirds
Water
1 egg, slightly beaten

2 tablespoons milk
Fine dry bread crumbs
Oil or shortening for frying

In medium saucepan, cover carrots with water. Bring to a boil and simmer about 5 minutes, or until almost done. Plunge carrots into cold water, then drain and pat dry with paper towels. In shallow bowl, mix egg and milk. Dip carrots in egg-milk mixture, then in bread crumbs. Fry in hot oil or shortening in mini-fryer for 2 minutes, or until golden. Makes 3 to 4 servings.

Marinated Cauliflower Fritters

Marinate cauliflower ahead of time, then fry just before serving.

1 small head cauliflower
Water, salted
1 cup red-wine-vinegar-and-oil
   salad dressing
1 cup flour
1 teaspoon baking powder

1/4 teaspoon salt
1 egg, slightly beaten
3/4 cup milk
Oil or shortening for frying
Grated Parmesan cheese

Break cauliflower into flowerets. Cook in salted water until done but firm, about 8 minutes. Drain. In medium bowl, pour dressing over cooked cauliflower. Marinate at least one hour. Drain thoroughly. In small bowl, combine flour, baking powder and salt. Stir in egg and milk. Mix until almost smooth. Dip drained cauliflower into batter. Drop into hot oil or shortening in mini-fryer. Fry until golden brown. Drain and sprinkle with grated Parmesan cheese. Serve hot. Makes 3 to 4 servings.

How to Make Marinated Cauliflower Fritters

Cook cauliflower until tender but firm. Drain and place in medium bowl. Pour salad dressing over cauliflower and let stand at least 1 hour to absorb flavors.

Be sure to drain marinated cauliflower thoroughly. With tongs, dip into prepared batter. Let excess drip off for a moment before frying.

After cauliflower fritters are fried in hot oil or shortening, sprinkle with grated Parmesan cheese.

Carrot Stacks

You'll never believe this terrific combination until you try it!

3 medium carrots, peeled
1 egg, slightly beaten
1/4 teaspoon salt
1 teaspoon brown sugar

1/4 teaspoon ground ginger
2 tablespoons flour
Oil or shortening for frying

Coarsely grate carrots. In medium bowl, combine egg, salt, brown sugar, ginger and flour. Stir in grated carrots. With teaspoon, pile mixture on another teaspoon, pressing slightly to make mixture more compact so carrots will not separate in frying. Drop by teaspoon into hot oil or shortening in mini-fryer. Fry about 2 minutes, until golden. Drain and serve hot. Makes 3 to 4 servings.

Corn Fritters

A favorite with chicken dinners!

1 (7-oz.) can whole-kernel corn
Milk
1-1/2 cups flour
1 tablespoon baking powder

3/4 teaspoon salt
1 egg, beaten
Oil or shortening for frying
Maple syrup

Drain corn, reserving liquid. Add enough milk to liquid to make 1 cup. In medium bowl, stir together flour, baking powder and salt. In small bowl, combine egg, milk mixture and corn. Stir into dry ingredients. Mix just until moistened. Drop batter by heaping tablespoons into hot oil or shortening in mini-fryer. Fry 1 to 1-1/2 minutes on each side, until golden brown. Drain. Serve hot with maple syrup. Makes 3 to 4 servings.

Farmland Corn Fritters

Quick and delicious!

2 cups biscuit mix
1/2 cup cold water
1 egg, slightly beaten
1 (17-oz.) can whole-kernel corn,
   drained

Oil or shortening for frying
Powdered sugar or maple syrup

In medium bowl, stir biscuit mix with cold water and egg until smooth. Add corn. Drop batter by teaspoon into hot oil or shortening in mini-fryer. Fry about 2-1/2 minutes or until golden brown and done in center. Drain. Sprinkle with powdered sugar or serve with maple syrup. Makes about 2 dozen fritters.

Fresh Corn Fritters

Lighter than most corn fritters—with a bacon flavor.

1 cup fresh corn kernels,
   cut from 1 large ear of corn
2 eggs, beaten
1/4 cup flour
1/2 teaspoon salt

1/8 teaspoon pepper
1 slice bacon, cooked until crisp,
   crumbled
1 tablespoon finely chopped green onion
Oil or shortening for frying

In medium bowl, combine corn with eggs, flour, salt, pepper, crumbled bacon and green onion. Carefully drop by tablespoon into hot oil or shortening in mini-fryer. Fry about 1-1/2 minutes or until golden. Drain. Serve hot. Makes 8 or 9 fritters.

Old-Fashioned French-Fried Onion Rings

Try this batter for French-fried zucchini or carrot slices.

1 egg
1 cup milk
1 tablespoon cooking oil
1 cup flour
1 teaspoon baking powder

1/4 teaspoon salt
3 onions
Oil or shortening for frying
Salt, if desired

In medium bowl, combine egg, milk and 1 tablespoon cooking oil. Add flour, baking powder and salt. Beat until smooth. Peel and slice onions in 1/4-inch-thick crosswise slices; separate into rings. Dip rings in batter. Fry in hot oil or shortening in mini-fryer until golden. Drain. Sprinkle with salt, if desired. Serve hot. Makes 4 to 5 servings.

Fried Green-Pepper Rings

Serve as a vegetable, or a garnish for roasts or steaks.

1 large green pepper
1/4 cup fine dry bread crumbs
2 tablespoons grated Parmesan cheese
1 teaspoon salt

1/8 teaspoon pepper
1 egg, beaten
2 tablespoons water
Oil or shortening for frying

Remove seeds and center of green pepper. Cut crosswise into 1/4-inch rings. In piepan, coat with a mixture of bread crumbs, grated Parmesan cheese, salt and pepper. In small bowl, dip in mixture of egg and water. Coat again with crumb mixture. Chill 1 hour. Drop 1 at a time into hot oil or shortening in mini-fryer. Fry about 1/2 minute until golden brown. Drain. Serve hot. Makes 2 servings.

Mexican Corn Fritters

South-of-the-Border flavor.

3 tablespoons flour
1/2 teaspoon baking powder
1/4 teaspoon salt
1/4 cup grated Parmesan cheese
1 egg, slightly beaten
1 cup drained corn, fresh,
  frozen or canned

1 tablespoon chopped pimiento
1 tablespoon chopped green onion
1 tablespoon chopped canned green chilies
Oil or shortening for frying

In medium bowl, combine flour, baking powder, salt and grated Parmesan cheese. Stir in egg, corn, pimiento, onion and chilies. Drop by heaping tablespoon into hot oil or shortening in mini-fryer. Fry about 1 minute on each side, until golden brown. Serve hot. Makes 12 fritters.

Corn Puffs

A light and puffy fritter.

2 egg yolks
1 cup drained corn, fresh,
  frozen or canned
1/4 teaspoon salt
1/8 teaspoon pepper

2 tablespoons flour
2 egg whites
Oil or shortening for frying
Honey or maple syrup, if desired

In medium bowl, beat egg yolks until light. Add corn, salt, pepper and flour. In small bowl, beat egg whites until stiff but not dry. Fold into corn mixture. Drop, about 1 tablespoon at a time, into hot oil or shortening in mini-fryer. Fry about 3 minutes until golden brown. Drain. Serve plain, or with honey or maple syrup, if desired. Makes 14 fritters.

Corny Corn Balls

Corn plus cornmeal gives the extra flavor.

1 cup flour
1/4 cup cornmeal
2 teaspoons baking powder
1/2 teaspoon baking soda
1/2 teaspoon salt

1 egg, beaten
1/4 cup dairy sour cream
1 (7-oz.) can cream-style corn
Oil or shortening for frying
Honey

In medium bowl, stir together flour, cornmeal, baking powder, baking soda and salt. Add egg, sour cream and corn. Stir until well-blended. Drop by tablespoon into hot oil or shortening in mini-fryer. Fry about 2-1/2 to 3-1/2 minutes, until golden brown. Drain. Serve warm with honey. Makes 16 to 20 corn balls.

French-Fried Eggplant

Dip it in bread, cracker or corn flake crumbs.

1 medium eggplant, peeled
Salt
1/2 cup flour
1 egg, slightly beaten

2 tablespoons milk
2/3 cup fine dry seasoned bread crumbs
Oil or shortening for frying

Cut eggplant into 1/2-inch crosswise slices; halve each slice. Sprinkle with salt. In shallow dish, dip eggplant in flour, then in small bowl, dip each slice in egg mixed with milk. In piepan, dip slices in seasoned bread crumbs. Drop into hot oil or shortening in mini-fryer. Fry about 1 minute on each side, until golden brown and tender. Drain and serve hot. Makes 4 to 5 servings.

Fried Okra

A Southern tradition!

1 lb. whole okra, fresh or frozen
Water
1 egg
1 tablespoon water
3/4 cup fine cracker crumbs

1/2 teaspoon salt
1/8 teaspoon pepper
Oil or shortening for frying
Creole Sauce, page 155, if desired

Place okra in a saucepan; cover with water. Cover pan and simmer 5 minutes. Drain and pat dry with paper towels. In small bowl, beat egg with 1 tablespoon water. In shallow dish, combine cracker crumbs with salt and pepper. Dip okra in egg mixture, then in crumbs. Fry in hot oil or shortening in mini-fryer about 2 minutes until golden brown. Drain. Serve hot. Good plain or with Creole Sauce, page 155, if desired. Makes 4 to 6 servings.

Heavenly Onion Rings

Beautiful every time—light and tender to eat.

2 medium onions
1 egg
1 cup buttermilk
1 cup flour

1/4 teaspoon salt
1/4 teaspoon seasoned salt
1/2 teaspoon baking soda
Oil or shortening for frying

Peel and slice onions 1/4-inch thick. Separate into rings. In medium bowl, beat egg with buttermilk. Add flour, salt, seasoned salt and baking soda. Stir until almost smooth. Dip onion rings in batter. Fry in hot oil or shortening in mini-fryer about 1 to 2 minutes until crisp and golden. Drain. Serve hot. Makes 3 to 4 servings.

Sweet-Potato Balls

A surprise in each center!

2 large cooked sweet potatoes
  (about 2 cups)
1/4 teaspoon salt
1 tablespoon brown sugar

6 large marshmallows, cut in half
1/4 cup melted butter or margarine
1/2 cup dry bread crumbs
Oil or shortening for frying

Peel and mash cooked sweet potatoes. In medium bowl, combine sweet potatoes with salt and brown sugar. Shape mixture into 12 balls around marshmallow halves. In shallow dish, roll balls in melted butter or margarine, then in piepan, roll in bread crumbs. Chill about 1 hour. Drop into hot oil or shortening in mini-fryer. Fry about 1-1/2 to 2 minutes, until golden brown. Drain. Serve hot. Makes 12 balls.

How to Make Sweet-Potato Balls

To shape mashed sweet potatoes around half of marshmallow, place part of mixture in hand, top with marshmallow, spoon remaining mixture over all. Lightly press into round shape.

Roll filled sweet-potato balls in melted butter, then in bread crumbs. Fry until golden brown.

See-Through Onion Rings

Just a scanty coating for these onions.

2 medium onions
1/2 cup evaporated milk, undiluted
1/2 cup flour

Oil or shortening for frying
Salt to taste

Peel onions and cut into 1/4-inch slices. Separate into rings. In small bowl, dip in milk, then in another bowl, dip slices in flour. Drop into oil or shortening in mini-fryer. Fry about 1-1/2 to 2 minutes until golden. Drain. Sprinkle with salt to taste. Serve hot. Makes 3 to 4 servings.

French-Fried Parsley

A real conversation piece!

1 large bunch parsley

Oil or shortening for frying

Break off parsley stems from clusters of leaves. Wash and thoroughly dry. If necessary, wrap in paper towels and leave in refrigerator several hours. Drop into hot oil or shortening in mini-fryer. Fry for just an instant until crisp. Parsley cooks very quickly so be careful not to overcook. Drain well. Use as a garnish for fried main dishes or vegetables.

Rice-and-Cheese Balls

Italian influence!

1/2 cup uncooked long-grain rice
2 tablespoons butter or margarine
2 tablespoons finely chopped onion
1/2 teaspoon seasoned salt
3/4 cup chicken broth or bouillon
1/4 cup dry white wine

2 tablespoons grated Parmesan cheese
2 eggs, slightly beaten
1 oz. mozzarella cheese,
    cut in 1/2-in. cubes
Fine dry bread crumbs
Oil or shortening for frying

In skillet, sauté rice in butter or margarine for several minutes. Stir in onion, seasoned salt, broth or bouillon and wine. Cover and simmer about 20 minutes until rice is tender. Remove from heat. Immediately stir in grated Parmesan cheese. In medium bowl, combine eggs with cooked rice mixture. Cover and refrigerate at least 1 hour. Scoop up 1 tablespoon rice mixture in a spoon. Place a cube of mozzarella cheese in the middle and then top with another spoonful of rice mixture. Press together to form a ball; if necessary, dip hands in bread crumbs to keep rice from sticking to them. In piepan, roll balls in bread crumbs. With slotted spoon or fryer basket, lower balls into hot oil or shortening in mini-fryer. Fry 1 minute until golden brown. Drain. Serve hot. Makes 10 balls.

Rice Fritters

A pleasant change from potatoes or plain rice.

1 cup flour
1-1/2 teaspoons baking powder
1/4 teaspoon salt
1 egg, slightly beaten
1 cup cooked rice

1/2 cup milk
1 green onion, finely chopped
2 tablespoons melted butter or margarine
Oil or shortening for frying
Grated Parmesan cheese

In small bowl, stir together flour, baking powder and salt. In medium bowl, combine egg, cooked rice, milk, green onion and butter or margarine. Add dry ingredients to egg mixture, stir just until flour is moistened. Drop batter by heaping teaspoons into hot oil or shortening in mini-fryer. Fry about 1-1/2 minutes on each side until golden brown. Drain. Sprinkle with grated Parmesan cheese while hot. Makes about 20 fritters.

How To Make Zucchini Fritters

Using grater with fairly large holes, grate unpeeled zucchini.

Opposite page shows vegetables you can use to make delectable taste treats in your mini-fryer. Zucchini rounds made from Zucchini Sticks recipe, page 116, are in lower part of photo.

Add grated zucchini to egg-yolk mixture before folding in beaten egg whites.

Pour grated cheese into small plastic bag; add 1 or 2 fritters. Shake bag to coat fritters.

Zucchini Sticks

Cut zucchini in thin rounds instead of sticks, if you prefer.

3 medium zucchini
3 tablespoons flour
1/4 teaspoon salt
1/8 teaspoon pepper
1/8 teaspoon garlic powder

2 eggs
2 tablespoons lemon juice
3/4 cup fine dry bread crumbs
Oil or shortening for frying
Salt or seasoned salt to taste

Cut zucchini into sticks about 1/2-inch thick. In shallow dish, mix flour with salt, pepper and garlic powder. Roll zucchini in flour mixture. In small bowl, beat eggs slightly with lemon juice. Dip flour-coated zucchini in egg mixture, then in piepan, dip zucchini in bread crumbs. Drop into hot oil or shortening in mini-fryer. Fry until golden brown. Drain. Serve hot. Sprinkle with salt or seasoned salt to taste. Makes 3 to 4 servings.

Zucchini Fritters

They puff into a variety of different shapes.

1 cup flour
1-1/2 teaspoons baking powder
1 teaspoon salt
2 teaspoons sugar
2 egg yolks
1/3 cup milk

1 tablespoon melted butter or margarine
1 cup finely grated,
   unpeeled zucchini
2 egg whites, stiffly beaten
Oil or shortening for frying
1/3 cup grated Parmesan cheese

In medium bowl, stir together flour, baking powder, salt and sugar. In small bowl, beat egg yolks well; add milk and melted butter or margarine. Stir egg mixture into dry ingredients. Carefully fold in zucchini and beaten egg whites. Drop by tablespoons into hot oil or shortening in mini-fryer. Fry about 1-1/2 minutes on each side. Drain. Shake fritters in a bag with grated Parmesan cheese. Serve hot. Makes 20 to 24 fritters.

Squash Drops

A new way to serve squash.

2 cups cooked, mashed acorn or
   banana squash
1 egg, beaten
1/3 cup flour

1/2 teaspoon baking powder
1/2 teaspoon salt
1/8 teaspoon nutmeg
Oil or shortening for frying

Mix cooked, mashed squash with egg, flour, baking powder, salt and nutmeg. Drop by teaspoons into hot oil or shortening in mini-fryer. Fry about 2 minutes until brown. Drain. Serve hot. Makes 24 to 26 drops.

Fried Sweet Potatoes

A change-of-pace potato dish!

2 medium sweet potatoes
Oil or shortening for frying
Salt to taste

Brown sugar, if desired
Nutmeg, if desired

Peel sweet potatoes and cut into 1/4-inch crosswise slices. Drop 2 to 4 at a time into hot oil or shortening in mini-fryer. Fry about 1-1/2 to 2 minutes until done. Drain on paper towels. Sprinkle lightly with salt to taste, then with brown sugar and nutmeg, if desired. Serve hot. Makes 30 to 45 slices, depending on size of potatoes.

Breads

As a method for cooking bread, frying is traditional for many favorite regional or ethnic breads. Hush puppies are favorites in the South, sopaipillas are popular in the Southwest and Indian fry bread is a contribution from the American Indian. All of these plus many more are just right for your mini-fryer.

The varieties range from quick breads to yeast breads; those made from a biscuit mix to those from frozen bread dough.

Small size is the common denominator. All are shaped to fit your mini-fryer. Sopaipillas, which have been popular in the Southwest for years, are just becoming known in other parts of the country. They are made from small squares or rectangles of dough. When dropped into hot oil or shortening, they puff up and become hollow in the center. There's no waiting around for bread to rise or long baking times. In fact, there's no yeast in sopaipillas; just a mixture of flour, baking powder, salt and shortening, with water stirred in. It's hard to believe that these ingredients, when combined and fried, could result in such marvelous golden puffs. Many people like to sprinkle sopaipillas with cinnamon and sugar and serve them instead of doughnuts, while others serve them as bread and pour honey over them or tear off a corner and pour honey inside.

Herb Puffs are well worth the extra time it takes to make yeast rolls from scratch. They are light, puffy, and delightfully herb flavored. Or try a shortcut to delicious fried bread with frozen bread dough. Garlic Cheese Rolls are aromatic, with a surprisingly pleasant flavor. Even if you omit the garlic, they will make a hit with everyone.

Cinnamon Blossoms

You'll like this short-cut with refrigerated biscuits.

1 (8-oz.) pkg. refrigerated biscuits
Oil or shortening for frying

1/4 cup sugar
1/4 teaspoon cinnamon

Separate biscuits. With scissors, make 5 cuts at regular intervals almost to center of each biscuit. Drop biscuits into hot oil or shortening in mini-fryer. Fry 1 minute on each side or until golden brown. Drain. Coat warm blossoms with mixture of sugar and cinnamon. Serve warm or cold. Makes 10 blossoms.

Herb Puffs

Try it for your next salad luncheon.

1 pkg. dry yeast
1/4 cup warm water,
    about 110°F, 43°C
1/3 cup milk
1 tablespoon sugar
3/4 teaspoon salt
1/4 teaspoon fines herbes

1/8 teaspoon dried dill weed
1 tablespoon shortening
1-3/4 to 2 cups flour
1 egg
Oil or shortening for frying
Butter or margarine

In small bowl, dissolve yeast in warm water. In small saucepan, heat milk, sugar, salt, fines herbes, dill weed and 1 tablespoon shortening until shortening starts to melt. In medium bowl, combine hot milk mixture, 1/2 cup of the flour, egg and dissolved yeast mixture. Beat well. Stir in remaining flour to form a moderately stiff, sticky dough. Place in large buttered bowl, cover and let rise in a warm place until doubled in bulk, about 45 minutes. Punch down. On lightly floured board, divide into 18 pieces, pat each into a 3-inch round. Let stand in a warm place for 1/2 hour. With slotted spoon or fryer basket, carefully lower into hot oil or shortening in mini-fryer. Fry about 1-1/2 to 2 minutes, until golden and puffy. Drain. Serve warm with butter or margarine. Makes 18 puffs.

Indian Fry-Bread

Resembles a miniature pita bread.

1 cup flour
3/4 teaspoon baking powder

1/3 cup plus 1 tablespoon milk
Oil or shortening for frying

In small bowl, mix flour, baking powder and milk. Form dough into ball. On lightly floured board, knead until smooth, about 3 to 4 minutes. In bowl, cover and let rise 30 minutes. Divide dough into 8 equal parts and shape in balls. On lightly floured board, roll each into a 3-inch circle, keeping remaining balls covered so dough does not dry out. Fry circles, one at a time, in hot oil or shortening in mini-fryer about 1 minute on each side until golden brown. Serve warm. Makes 8 servings.

Garlic-Cheese Rolls

Tasting is believing!

1 (16-oz.) loaf frozen bread dough
Oil or shortening for frying
1/3 cup melted butter or margarine

1 clove garlic, mashed
1/2 cup grated Parmesan cheese

Thaw bread according to package directions. On lightly floured board, divide into 18 balls. Cover and let stand about 15 minutes. Roll out each bread ball to a 4-inch circle. Fold in sides of dough, then roll up, pinching seams to seal. Place seam-side-down on lightly buttered cookie sheets. Cover and let rise until almost doubled in bulk, about 1 to 1-1/2 hours. Fry in hot oil or shortening in mini-fryer for 1-1/2 to 2-1/2 minutes or until brown. Drain. In small bowl, combine butter or margarine and garlic. Dip warm rolls into garlic mixture, then in grated Parmesan cheese. Serve hot. Makes 18 rolls.

Puffy Health Bread

Good whole-wheat flavor!

1 cup whole-wheat flour	1/2 cup unflavored yogurt
1/4 teaspoon salt	Oil or shortening for frying

In medium bowl, mix whole-wheat flour, salt and yogurt until well-blended. Shape into 12 balls. On lightly floured board, roll into 3-1/2- to 4-inch rounds. Fry in hot oil or shortening in mini-fryer about 1 to 1-1/2 minutes, until puffy and brown. Drain. Serve warm. Makes 12 rolls.

Fried Cracker Bread

Crisp and bubbly like Armenian cracker bread.

1 pkg. dry yeast	About 4 cups flour
1-1/2 cups warm water	1/4 cup toasted sesame seeds
1 teaspoon salt	Oil or shortening for frying

In large bowl, stir yeast in warm water until dissolved. Add salt and enough flour to make stiff dough. Turn onto lightly floured board and knead until smooth and elastic, about 8 to 10 minutes. Shape into ball; put in buttered bowl and turn dough to butter top. Cover and let rise in a warm place until doubled in bulk, about 1-1/2 hours. Punch down and let rise again, about 1/2 hour. Pinch off a ball of dough about 1-1/2 inches in diameter and roll out to about 3-inch disk on lightly floured board sprinkled with sesame seeds. Drop one at a time into hot oil or shortening in mini-fryer. Fry about 1 minute on each side. Drain. Serve warm or cold. Makes about 25 servings.

How To Make
Fried Onion Buns

After adding other ingredients, stir enough flour into yeast mixture to make a stiff dough.

When dough has risen, break off a 2-inch piece of dough for each bun.

With fingers, pat out each piece of dough into a 3-inch round.

Onion Hush Puppies

Onion-flavored hush puppies may become a new tradition!

3/4 cup cornmeal
1/2 cup flour
3/4 teaspoon baking soda
1/2 teaspoon salt
1 egg, beaten

1/2 cup buttermilk
1/3 cup finely chopped onion
Oil or shortening for frying
Fish, if desired

In medium bowl, combine cornmeal, flour, baking soda and salt. Add egg and buttermilk; mix well. Stir in onion. Drop by teaspoons into hot oil or shortening in mini-fryer. Fry about 2 to 2-1/2 minutes, until golden brown. Drain. Serve hot with fish, if desired. Makes 18 to 20 hush puppies.

Fried Onion Buns

These savory buns are great with barbecued beef or ribs.

1 large onion, minced
3 tablespoons butter or margarine
3/4 cup milk, scalded
1 teaspoon honey
1 teaspoon salt
1/2 teaspoon coarsely ground pepper

1/2 teaspoon celery salt
1 pkg. dry yeast
1/4 cup warm water,
   about 110°F (43°C)
2-3/4 to 3 cups flour
Oil or shortening for frying

In small saucepan or skillet, sauté onion in 1 tablespoon of the butter or margarine. Place remaining 2 tablespoons butter or margarine in medium bowl. Pour hot milk over butter or margarine in bowl. Add honey, salt, pepper and celery salt. Stir until butter or margarine melts. Cool to lukewarm. In 1-cup measure, sprinkle yeast over warm water, and stir until dissolved. Let stand in a warm place about 10 minutes. Stir sautéed onions and dissolved yeast mixture into lukewarm milk mixture. Add 1/2 of flour to milk mixture. Beat for 3 minutes. With spoon, stir in enough of remaining flour to make stiff dough. Turn dough out on lightly floured board. Knead about 5 minutes, or until elastic. Put in large buttered bowl and turn dough to butter top. Cover and let rise until doubled in bulk, about 1-1/2 hours. Punch down. Separate dough into 2-inch pieces and pat out to 3-inch diameter circles. Drop into hot oil or shortening in mini-fryer. Fry until golden brown. Drain. Serve warm. Makes 1-1/2 dozen buns.

Variation:

To make Cream-Cheese Turnovers, combine 2 ounces soft cream cheese, 1/4 cup sour cream and 2 slices cooked, crumbled bacon. Set aside. Follow directions for making onion buns, except separate dough into 1-inch pieces. On lightly floured board, roll out to 3-inch diameter. Spread about 2 teaspoons cream-cheese filling over 1/2 of each round. Fold over to enclose filling. Pinch edges to seal. Fry in hot oil or shortening in mini-fryer until golden brown. Serve warm. Makes 30 to 35 small turnovers.

Fried Biscuits

The Southern complement to chicken and gravy!

1/2 cup flour
1 teaspoon baking powder
1/8 teaspoon salt
1 tablespoon butter or margarine,
   cut in bits

3 tablespoons milk
Oil or shortening for frying
Fried chicken and gravy, if desired

In medium bowl, combine flour with baking powder and salt. With pastry blender or fork, cut in butter or margarine until mixture resembles coarse crumbs. Pour in milk and mix with fork. Shape dough into ball. On lightly floured board, roll out 1/4-inch thick. Cut into 1-1/2-inch rounds. Drop 1 or 2 at a time into hot oil or shortening in mini-fryer. Fry about 1 minute on each side, until evenly browned. Drain. Serve hot with fried chicken and gravy, if desired. Makes 10 biscuits.

Crunchy Rounds

Crisp like a cracker—light and puffy like a hollow biscuit.

1-1/2 cups flour
1/2 cup cornmeal
1-1/2 teaspoons salt
1-1/2 teaspoons dry mustard
1/2 teaspoon baking soda

1/3 cup shortening
1 tablespoon prepared horseradish
1/3 cup sour cream
Oil or shortening for frying

In medium bowl, combine flour, cornmeal, salt, dry mustard and baking soda. Cut in 1/3 cup shortening and horseradish until mixture resembles coarse crumbs. Stir in sour cream. On lightly floured board, knead dough several times. Roll out about 1/8-inch thick. Cut with biscuit cutter. Drop into hot oil or shortening in mini-fryer. Fry about 2 minutes until puffy and golden. Drain. Serve warm or cool. Makes 28 to 32 rounds.

Shortcut Hush Puppies

Good texture with popular cornmeal crunch.

1 cup biscuit mix
1 cup cornmeal
1 teaspoon salt

1 egg, slightly beaten
3/4 cup milk
Oil or shortening for frying

In medium bowl, combine biscuit mix, cornmeal, salt, egg and milk. Drop batter by teaspoons into hot oil or shortening in mini-fryer. Fry about 2 to 2-1/2 minutes, until brown. Drain. Serve hot. Makes 15 to 20 hush puppies.

Yam Buns

A conversation-starter for your next salad luncheon.

1 (3/4 cup) small yam or sweet potato,
  cooked and peeled
2 tablespoons butter or
  margarine, softened
1/2 cup milk, scalded
1 cup all-purpose flour
1 cup whole-wheat flour

1/2 cup brown sugar
1/2 teaspoon salt
2 teaspoons baking powder
1/2 teaspoon cinnamon
1/4 teaspoon nutmeg
Oil or shortening for frying

In large bowl, mash yam or sweet potato with butter or margarine; stir in hot milk. In medium bowl, combine flours with brown sugar, salt, baking powder, cinnamon and nutmeg. Stir into yam mixture. Mix well. Cover and refrigerate at least 1 hour. On lightly floured board, pat out chilled dough about 1/8-inch thick. Cut with floured biscuit cutter. Drop into hot oil or shortening in mini-fryer. Fry about 1-1/2 to 2 minutes, until golden brown. Drain. Serve warm. Makes 20 to 30 buns.

Sopaipillas

Little pillow-shaped puffs, so light they melt in your mouth.

1 cup flour
1-1/2 teaspoon baking powder
1/4 teaspoon salt
1 tablespoon shortening

1/3 cup water
Oil or shortening for frying
Honey and butter, if desired
Cinnamon and sugar, if desired

In medium bowl, stir together flour, baking powder and salt. Cut in 1 tablespoon shortening with pastry blender or fork until mixture resembles cornmeal. Gradually add water, stirring with fork. Turn out on lightly floured board. Knead into smooth ball. Divide in half, let stand 10 minutes. Roll out each half to 10" x 12" rectangle. Cut into 2" x 3" rectangles. Do not re-roll or patch dough. Drop 1 or 2 at a time into hot oil or shortening in mini-fryer. Fry about 1 minute on each side until golden. Drain. Serve hot with honey and butter, or roll in cinnamon and sugar. Makes 20 sopaipillas.

Buñuelos

Mexicans make this version of puffy fried bread.

2 cups flour
2 teaspoons sugar
1/2 teaspoon baking powder
1/4 teaspoon salt
1 egg

1/3 cup milk
2 tablespoons melted butter
Oil or shortening for frying
Cinnamon
Sugar

In medium bowl, combine flour, sugar, baking powder and salt. Add egg, milk and melted butter. Mix to form a soft dough. On lightly floured board, knead about 2 minutes or until smooth. Divide into 24 balls. Cover and let stand 1/2 hour. Roll out to 3-1/2- to 4-inch rounds. Drop into hot oil or shortening in mini-fryer. Fry 1 to 1-1/2 minutes or until golden brown and puffy. Drain. Sprinkle with cinnamon and sugar. Serve warm. Makes 24 buñuelos.

Sopaipillas

Deep-Fried Croutons

A quickie to fix while the mini-fryer is still hot!

2 slices bread
Oil or shortening for frying

Seasoned salt or herb seasoning

Trim crust off bread. Cut bread into 1/2-inch cubes. Drop 1/2 of cubes into hot oil or shortening in mini-fryer. Fry about 1/2 minute until golden brown, moving croutons around constantly with slotted spoon. Drain. Sprinkle with seasoned salt or herb seasoning. Use as a topping for soups or green salads.

Hush Puppies

Corn-bread mixture goes great with fried fish.

1-1/2 cups cornmeal
1/2 cup flour
2 teaspoons baking powder
1 teaspoon salt

1 egg, slightly beaten
3/4 cup milk
Oil or shortening for frying

In medium bowl, combine cornmeal, flour, baking powder and salt. In small bowl, mix egg and milk. Stir into dry ingredients until just moistened. Drop by tablespoons into hot oil or shortening in mini-fryer. Fry about 2 minutes on each side, until golden brown. Drain. Serve hot. Makes 14 to 16 hush puppies.

Desserts

Fried desserts are great when you want something special to top off a memorable meal. For a really different idea, try Funnel Cake—an updated version of the traditional Pennsylvania-Dutch dish. It is called Funnel Cake because you pour batter through a funnel into hot oil or shortening. It takes the shape of your mini-fryer and has the appearance of a maze created by the crisscrossing pattern of the batter. After it is fried and drained, you can sprinkle it with powdered sugar and eat it "as is." The texture is something like a waffle so it is also delicious when topped with sweetened strawberries or blueberries and sour cream.

Swedish Rosettes are my favorite. They are so delicate, yet crisp and golden. It is necessary to have a rosette iron to make these shapes. These irons are available in gourmet shops, department stores, hardware and discount stores. Just heat the iron, dip into the batter and fry. Sprinkle with powdered sugar and you'll marvel at these party-pretty rosettes.

Fruits are very prominent in fried desserts. You can slice and coat them with various crumb mixtures or you can chop them and mix into a fritter batter.

Most fruits are rather juicy so it is important to pour off liquid, then pat dry with paper towels. This enables the coating to stick more securely and helps them fry properly.

When dropping fruit fritters into hot oil or shortening, be sure to use the approximate amount that is suggested in the recipe. If you make them too large, it is difficult to get them done in the center, without being overcooked on the outside.

Drop them very gently, and fry 2 to 4 at a time, depending on the diameter of your mini-fryer. Turn them over when golden on one side, although some will turn themselves; then lift out with slotted metal spoon or mini-basket.

Traditional Banana Fritters

Serve banana fritters plain or with a fancy sauce!

4 bananas
1 tablespoon lemon juice
2 tablespoons sifted powdered sugar
1/2 cup biscuit mix
1 tablespoon sugar

1 egg, slightly beaten
1/4 cup milk
Oil or shortening for frying
Sifted powdered sugar
Maple syrup or fruit sauce, if desired

Peel bananas, cut each into 4 chunks. Sprinkle with lemon juice, then 2 tablespoons powdered sugar. Set aside while making batter. In small bowl, combine biscuit mix, sugar, egg and milk. Beat with a spoon or whisk until almost smooth. Dip banana chunks in batter. Gently drop into hot oil or shortening in mini-fryer. Fry 1 to 1-1/2 minutes, or until golden. Drain. Serve warm, sprinkled with powdered sugar. Serve with maple syrup or fruit sauce, if desired. Makes 4 to 5 fritters.

Brandied Banana Fritters

A grand finale to any special dinner.

4 bananas
3 tablespoons sifted powdered sugar
1/4 cup brandy
1 teaspoon grated lemon peel
1 cup flour
1 teaspoon baking powder

1/4 teaspoon salt
1 egg, separated
2/3 cup milk
1 teaspoon melted butter
Oil or shortening for frying
Whipped cream, maple syrup or brandy sauce

Peel bananas. Cut each into 4 crosswise pieces, then cut each piece in 1/2 lengthwise. In small bowl, stir together powdered sugar, brandy and grated lemon peel. Pour over bananas and marinate about 1/2 hour. In small bowl, combine flour, baking powder and salt. In another bowl, beat egg white until stiff. In medium bowl, beat egg yolk until light yellow; stir in milk and melted butter. Stir in flour mixture, then 1 tablespoon of brandy mixture in which bananas are marinating. Fold in egg white. Drain bananas thoroughly, dip into batter. Drop into hot oil or shortening in mini-fryer. Fry 1 to 2 minutes, until golden brown. Drain. Serve warm with whipped cream, maple syrup or brandy sauce. Makes 5 to 6 fritters.

Blueberry Fritters

A light batter, dotted with blueberries.

2 tablespoons sugar
1 cup frozen blueberries
1 cup flour
1 teaspoon baking powder
1/4 teaspoon nutmeg
1/4 teaspoon grated orange peel

1/4 teaspoon salt
1 egg, slightly beaten
1/4 cup milk
Oil or shortening for frying
Sifted powdered sugar

Sprinkle sugar over frozen berries. Let stand about 1 hour. Drain well. In medium bowl, mix flour, baking powder, nutmeg, grated orange peel and salt. Add egg and milk. Beat until smooth. Carefully fold in drained berries. Drop about one tablespoon mixture at a time into hot oil or shortening in mini-fryer. Fry about 2 to 2-1/2 minutes, or until golden brown and done inside. Drain. Sprinkle generously with powdered sugar. Serve warm. Makes 12 to 14 fritters.

Caribbean Banana Fritters

Yummy ginger-rum sauce!

3 bananas
1 tablespoon sugar
1/8 teaspoon ground ginger
1/4 cup rum
2 eggs, separated
2/3 cup milk

1 tablespoon melted butter
1 cup flour
1/4 teaspoon salt
Oil or shortening for frying
1/2 cup sugar

Peel bananas. Cut each into 1-inch crosswise slices. Place in medium bowl. Sprinkle with 1 tablespoon sugar and ginger. Pour rum over all. Let stand about 1/2 hour. Drain bananas, reserving marinade. In large bowl, beat egg yolks until light yellow. Add milk and melted butter. Stir in flour and salt. Beat until smooth. In small bowl, beat egg whites until stiff. Fold into batter. Dip well-drained bananas into batter. Drop into hot oil or shortening in mini-fryer. Fry about 1 to 2 minutes, until brown. Drain. In small saucepan add 1/2 cup sugar to reserved marinade. Heat until sugar dissolves. Brush hot cooked fritters with sauce. Serve hot. Makes about 15 fritters.

Cherry Twists El Charro

A delightful dessert inspired by Tucson's El Charro Restaurant.

10 to 12 cooked Basic Crepes,
   freshly made or frozen, see below
1 (20-oz.) can cherry or berry pie filling
1 egg, slightly beaten

1 tablespoon water
Oil or shortening for frying
Sifted powdered sugar

Basic Crepes:
4 eggs
1/4 teaspoon salt
2 cups flour

2-1/4 cups milk
2 tablespoons melted butter

Prepare Basic Crepes. Place one tablespoon pie filling on lower third of each crepe. Brush bottom and top edges of crepe with egg mixed with water. Fold right and left sides of crepe over filling, then roll up. Carefully lower crepe (seam side down) into hot oil or shortening in mini-fryer. Fry about 1 minute, until crisp and golden. Drain. Sprinkle with powdered sugar and spoon extra filling over top. Makes 10 to 12 cherry crepes.

Basic Crepes:

In medium bowl, combine eggs and salt. Gradually add flour alternately with milk; beat with an electric mixer or whisk until smooth. Beat in melted butter. If blender is used, combine ingredients in blender jar and blend about 1 minute. Scrape down sides with rubber spatula and blend for another 15 seconds. If possible, let stand 1 hour. Cook on upside-down crepe griddle or in traditional crepe pan. Makes 30 to 35 crepes. Freeze extra crepes for future use.

Variation:

Substitute flour tortillas for crepes, using a wedge-shaped portion of tortilla.

Substitute apples or other fruits for filling and add a dollop of whipped cream as a topping. Sprinkle cinnamon on top of whipped cream.

Ambrosia Fritters

Texture like a delicate orange-coconut cake.

1 egg
1/4 cup sugar
1 teaspoon grated orange peel
1 tablespoon shortening
1 cup flour
1 teaspoon baking powder

1/4 teaspoon salt
1/4 cup orange juice
1/3 cup flaked coconut
Oil or shortening for frying
Orange Glaze, see below

Orange Glaze:
1 cup sifted powdered sugar
2 tablespoons orange liqueur

In medium bowl, beat egg until light and foamy. Beat in sugar, grated orange peel and 1 tablespoon shortening. In small bowl, combine flour, baking powder and salt alternately with orange juice. Add flour mixture to egg mixture. Stir in coconut. Drop by teaspoons into hot oil or shortening in mini-fryer. Fry about 2 to 3 minutes, or until brown. Drain. Dip into Orange Glaze while warm. Makes 14 fritters.

Orange Glaze:
Combine powdered sugar with orange liqueur. Blend well.

Crunchy Strawberry Surprise

Crunchy on the outside, juicy on the inside!

1/2 cup apricot jam or preserves
1 pt. fresh strawberries
1/2 cup ground walnuts
2 eggs, slightly beaten

1/2 cup finely crushed vanilla wafers
Oil or shortening for frying
Sifted powdered sugar

Press jam or preserves through sieve into small bowl. Wash and hull strawberries; if berries with long stems are available, do not hull, but dip in coatings by stems. Carefully pat dry with paper towels. Dip in preserves, using fork to help completely coat berries. Allow excess to drip through fork tines. Coat with nuts. Shake gently. In another small bowl, dip berries in beaten eggs, smoothing off excess. Coat berries with crushed vanilla wafers. Place on wire rack. Chill 30 minutes to set coating. Carefully drop berries into hot oil or shortening in mini-fryer. Fry until golden brown. Drain. Sprinkle with powdered sugar. Serve as soon as berries have cooled enough to eat. Makes enough coating for 15 to 25 strawberries, depending on size.

French-Fried Strawberries

Let everyone dip their own strawberries!

1 pt. fresh strawberries
1 egg, beaten
1/2 cup milk
2 tablespoons sugar
1/2 teaspoon baking powder
1 teaspoon melted butter or margarine

1/2 teaspoon vanilla
3/4 cup flour
Oil or shortening for frying
1/3 cup dairy sour cream
1/3 cup flaked coconut

Wash and hull strawberries. Gently pat dry with paper towels. In small mixing bowl, combine egg and milk. Stir in sugar, baking powder, butter or margarine, vanilla and flour. Beat until smooth. Spear berries with fondue forks or skewers and dip in batter. Fry in hot oil or shortening in mini-fryer until batter is golden. Drain. Serve as soon as berries have cooled enough to eat. Dip in sour cream, then coconut. Makes enough batter for 15 to 25 strawberries, depending on size.

Hawaiian Fruit-Balls

A treat from the tropics!

1 cup flour
1 teaspoon baking powder
1 teaspoon salt
2 eggs
1/2 cup milk
1 teaspoon cooking oil

1 teaspoon grated orange peel
1/2 cup canned sliced pineapple,
   well-drained, cut in small pieces
1/2 cup diced bananas
Oil or shortening for frying
Coconut Glaze, see below

Coconut Glaze:
1 cup sifted powdered sugar
1-1/2 tablespoons milk

1 cup flaked coconut

In medium bowl, stir together flour, baking powder, and salt. Add eggs, 1/2 cup milk and 1 teaspoon oil. Beat with rotary beater until smooth. Stir in grated orange peel, pineapple and banana pieces. Drop by tablespoons into hot oil or shortening in mini-fryer. Fry about 2 minutes or until golden. Drain. Makes 22 to 24 balls.

Coconut Glaze:
Mix powdered sugar and 1-1/2 tablespoons milk. Dip warm fruit balls in sugar glaze, then in coconut.

Hold finger over end of funnel spout while pouring batter into top of funnel.

How to Make Funnel Cakes

Move the funnel in a crisscross pattern above the surface of the oil.

Cooked funnel cake will resemble a maze of "curly" golden-brown cake.

Funnel Cakes

Amaze them all when you make this maze!

1 egg
3/4 cup milk
1-1/4 cup flour
2 tablespoons sugar
1 teaspoon baking soda

3/4 teaspoon baking powder
1/4 teaspoon salt
Oil or shortening for frying
Sifted powdered sugar
Strawberries, blueberries or maple syrup, if desired

In medium bowl, beat egg with milk, flour, sugar, baking soda, baking powder and salt. Using funnel with about 3/8-inch-diameter spout opening, hold finger over end of funnel spout. Pour about 3 tablespoons batter into funnel if using round mini-fryer, or 4 tablespoons batter for rectangular mini-fryer. Hold funnel above mini-fryer; move finger. As batter flows through spout, move funnel in a crisscrossing pattern above surface of hot oil or shortening until funnel is empty. Batter should drip rapidly through funnel spout; if too thick, add 1 to 1-1/2 tablespoons milk. Cake will take shape of mini-fryer. Fry about 1 minute; turn and fry about 1/2 minute. Drain. Sprinkle with powdered sugar. Serve warm. Good plain, or with strawberries, blueberries or maple syrup, if desired. Makes about 6 cakes, depending on size of mini-fryer.

Date Won Ton

This is extra quick with frozen won ton skins.

1/2 cup chopped dates
1 tablespoon crunchy peanut butter
1 teaspoon grated orange peel

9 won ton skins or wrappers
Oil or shortening for frying
Sifted powdered sugar

In small bowl, mix dates with peanut butter and grated orange peel. Place about 1 rounded teaspoon of filling in center of each won ton skin. Moisten edges of skin. Fold 2 opposite corners together, forming a triangle. Seal edges. Pull right and left corners of folded triangle down and below folded edge so they slightly overlap. Moisten overlapping corners and pinch together. Fry in hot oil or shortening in mini-fryer about 1 minute, or until crisp and golden. Drain. Sprinkle with powdered sugar. Makes 9 won ton.

Note:
Won ton skins or wrappers are available in oriental markets, gourmet shops and the frozen food or deli sections of many supermarkets.

Fig-Nut Won Ton

A different shortcut dessert.

1/2 cup chopped dried figs
1/4 cup chopped walnuts
1 tablespoon lemon juice
1/2 teaspoon grated lemon peel

15 won ton skins or wrappers
Oil or shortening for frying
Sifted powdered sugar

In small bowl, combine figs, walnuts, lemon juice and grated lemon peel. Place about 1 rounded teaspoon of mixture in center of won ton skin. Moisten edges of skin. Fold 2 opposite corners together, forming a triangle. Seal edges. Pull the right and left corners of folded triangle down and below folded edge so they slightly overlap. Moisten overlapping corners and pinch together. Fry in hot oil or shortening in mini-fryer about 1 minute, or until crisp and golden. Drain. Sprinkle with powdered sugar. Serve warm or cool. Makes 15 won ton.

Note:
Won ton skins or wrappers are available in Oriental markets, gourmet shops and the frozen-food or deli sections of many supermarkets.

Blintzes With Wine-Berry Sauce

Freeze crepes ahead and make these in a jiffy!

1 cup *dry* cottage cheese
1 (3-oz.) pkg. cream cheese, softened
1/2 teaspoon grated lemon peel
2 tablespoons sugar
8 to 10 Basic Crepes, page 133

1 egg
1 tablespoon water
Oil or shortening for frying
Wine-Berry Sauce, see below

Wine-Berry Sauce:
1 cup seedless raspberry or
   blackberry preserves

1 teaspoon lemon juice
2 tablespoons port wine

In small bowl, combine dry cottage cheese, cream cheese, grated lemon peel and sugar. Mix thoroughly. Place about 2 tablespoons mixture in center of each crepe. Brush edges of crepe with egg beaten with water. Fold over bottom, both sides and top. With slotted spoon or fryer basket, carefully lower 2 or 3 at a time into hot oil or shortening in mini-fryer. Fry about 1 to 1-1/2 minutes, or until crisp and golden. Drain and serve warm with Wine-Berry Sauce. Makes 8 to 10 blintzes.

Wine-Berry Sauce:
In small saucepan, heat preserves with lemon juice until mixture bubbles. Stir in wine.

Soufflé Fritters

The ultimate in elegant desserts!

1/4 cup butter
1/2 cup water
1/2 cup flour
2 eggs

1 tablespoon brandy or orange liqueur
Oil or shortening for frying
Sifted powdered sugar
Raspberry Sauce, see below

Raspberry Sauce:
1 (10-oz.) pkg. frozen raspberries
1 tablespoon sugar

2 tablespoons cornstarch
2 tablespoons port wine

In saucepan, heat butter and water until butter melts and mixture boils. Remove from heat. Add flour all at once and beat vigorously with wooden spoon until well-blended. Return pan to medium heat, beating constantly, about 1 minute or until mixture clings to spoon from bottom and sides of pan. Remove from heat and let stand 5 to 6 minutes. Make a well in center of dough. Drop in 1 egg and beat vigorously. Beat in other egg until smooth and glossy. Add brandy or orange liqueur. Drop by teaspoons into hot oil or shortening in mini-fryer. Fry about 4 to 5 minutes, or until very puffy and brown. Drain. Sprinkle with powdered sugar. Serve immediately with Raspberry Sauce. Makes about 10 to 12 fritters.

Raspberry Sauce:
Partially thaw raspberries. In small saucepan, combine sugar and cornstarch. Stir in raspberries with juice. Cook over low heat, stirring until thick. Remove from heat. Stir in wine. Blend well.

Swedish Rosettes

A Rosette Iron makes these delicate party treats.

1 egg
1 tablespoon sugar
1/2 cup milk
1/2 cup flour

1/4 teaspoon salt
1 teaspoon vanilla
Oil or shortening for frying
Sifted powdered sugar

In medium bowl, beat egg. Add sugar and milk. Stir in flour and salt, and beat until smooth. Add vanilla. Heat rosette iron by dipping it in hot oil or shortening in mini-fryer. Quickly drain excess oil on paper towels so iron stays hot. Immediately dip iron into batter, to not more than 3/4 the depth of rosette iron. If only a thin layer adheres to rosette iron, dip again immediately. Plunge batter-coated iron into hot oil or shortening in mini-fryer. Fry until active bubbling ceases. With fork, ease rosette off iron onto paper towels. While warm, sprinkle with powdered sugar. Makes 2 to 3 dozen rosettes.

Note:
Rosette irons are available with other kitchen utensils in department stores, gourmet kitchen shops, hardware and discount stores.

Before dipping rosette iron into batter, dip in hot oil; quickly drain excess oil on towels. If you change to star or butterfly shape, don't forget to heat it, too.

Dip preheated rosette iron in batter immediately after heating it in oil. Do not immerse more than 3/4 the depth of rosette iron.

How to Make Swedish Rosettes

Plunge batter-coated iron into mini-fryer until completely covered with hot oil. Lots of bubbles will appear on oil. Remove when active bubbling ceases or when rosette is golden.

Hold fried rosette over several layers of paper towels. Sometimes rosettes will fall off. If not, ease off with fork. Sprinkle with powdered sugar while warm.

Ricotta Puffs

Serve as a snack, dessert, or even for breakfast.

1/2 cup ricotta cheese
2 eggs
2 tablespoons sugar
1/2 cup flour
2 teaspoons baking powder

1/8 teaspoon salt
Oil or shortening for frying
Sifted powdered sugar
Jam or jelly, if desired

In medium bowl, beat cheese, eggs, and sugar with a wooden spoon until smooth. In small bowl, stir together flour, baking powder and salt. Beat flour mixture into cheese mixture to form a smooth thick batter. Drop batter by rounded teaspoons into hot oil or shortening in mini-fryer. Fry until golden brown, about 1 minute on each side. Just before serving sift powdered sugar over top. Serve warm. Good plain or with jam or jelly. Makes 16 to 18 puffs.

Greek Honey Puffs

Light and delicate in texture and flavor.

3/4 cup unflavored yogurt
1/2 teaspoon grated lemon peel
1 egg yolk
1 tablespoon melted butter
1 cup flour
2 tablespoons sugar

1 teaspoon baking powder
1/2 teaspoon baking soda
1/4 teaspoon salt
1 egg white
Honey

In medium bowl, mix yogurt, grated lemon peel, egg yolk and butter. Stir in flour, sugar, baking powder, baking soda and salt. In small bowl, beat egg white until stiff, but not dry. Fold into yogurt mixture. Drop by teaspoon into hot oil or shortening in mini-fryer. Fry in hot oil or shortening in mini-fryer about 2 minutes until golden brown. Drain. Serve warm with honey. Makes 20 to 25 puffs.

Apple Rings

You might like these spicy rings better than apple pie.

2 large cooking apples
1 cup flour
2 tablespoons sugar
1 teaspoon baking powder
Dash salt
1 egg, beaten

1 teaspoon cooking oil
2/3 cup milk
Oil or shortening for frying
1/4 cup sugar
1/2 teaspoon cinnamon

Core, peel and slice apples in rings about 1/4-inch thick. In medium bowl, thoroughly mix flour, margarine, sugar, baking powder and salt. Combine egg, 1 teaspoon oil and milk; add, all at once, to dry ingredients, stirring just until blended. Dip apple rings in batter, 1 at a time. Fry in hot oil or shortening in mini-fryer until brown, about 1 minute on each side. Drain. Sprinkle warm rings with sugar and cinnamon mixture. Serve warm. Makes 4 to 5 servings.

Apple-Spice Rings

These rings have a spicy surprise inside!

2 cooking apples
3/4 cup flour
1 tablespoon sugar
1/8 teaspoon salt
1 egg, separated

1/4 cup milk
2 tablespoons sugar
1/2 teaspoon cinnamon
Oil or shortening for frying

Core and peel apples. Slice in rings 1/4- to 1/3-inch thick. In medium bowl, stir together flour, 1 tablespoon sugar and salt. In small bowl, beat together egg yolk and milk. In another bowl, beat egg white until stiff. Stir egg-yolk mixture into dry ingredients, mixing until smooth. Fold egg white into mixture. In shallow dish, combine 2 tablespoons sugar and cinnamon. Dip apple rings in cinnamon-sugar mixture, then in batter, coating thoroughly. Fry in hot oil or shortening in mini-fryer for 3 to 4 minutes, or until golden brown and apples are done. Serve warm. Makes 4 to 5 servings.

Apple Fritters

Great with a cup of coffee or glass of milk!

1 cup flour
1 teaspoon baking powder
1/4 teaspoon nutmeg
1/2 teaspoon salt
2 tablespoons sugar
2 eggs

1/3 cup milk
1 large cooking apple, peeled and chopped
Oil or shortening for frying
1/2 cup sugar
1 teaspoon cinnamon

In medium bowl, combine flour, baking powder, nutmeg, salt and 2 tablespoons sugar. Add eggs and milk. Beat with rotary beater until smooth. Stir in apples. Drop tablespoons of batter mixture into hot oil or shortening in mini-fryer. Fry about 2-1/2 to 3 minutes, or until brown and done inside. Drain. While warm, roll in combination of 1/2 cup sugar and cinnamon. Makes about 18 fritters.

Rosy Cinnamon-Apple Rings

You'll want to try this with fresh pears, too!

1 egg, slightly beaten
1 cup milk
1 tablespoon cooking oil
1 tablespoon sugar
1 cup flour

1 teaspoon baking powder
1/4 teaspoon salt
2 large cooking apples
Oil or shortening for frying
Cinnamon Sauce, see below

Cinnamon Sauce:
1 cup water
1/4 cup sugar

2 teaspoons cornstarch
1/4 cup red cinnamon candies

In medium mixing bowl, combine egg, milk and 1 tablespoon oil. Add sugar, flour, baking powder and salt. Beat until smooth. Core, peel and slice apples in rings about 1/4-inch thick. Dip rings in batter, 1 at a time. Fry in hot oil or shortening in mini-fryer until golden, about 1 minute on each side. Drain. Serve warm with Cinnamon Sauce. Makes 4 servings.

Cinnamon Sauce:
In small saucepan, combine water, sugar and cornstarch. Bring to a boil. Pour in candies; stir until melted. Serve with apple rings.

How to Make Rosy Cinnamon-Apple Rings

After sauce for apples is thickened, spoon in cinnamon candies; stir until melted.

To make apple rings, core and peel apples; slice crosswise into 1/4-inch-thick rings.

Dip rings in batter; fry until golden. Pour warm cinnamon sauce over rings.

Knotted Pastry Ribbons

The shape is intriguing, yet simple.

1-1/2 cups flour
1/4 cup cooking oil
1 tablespoon sugar
1 egg

1 tablespoon dry white wine
1/4 teaspoon salt
Oil or shortening for frying
Sifted powdered sugar

In medium bowl, combine flour, 1/4 cup cooking oil, sugar, egg, wine and salt. On lightly floured board, knead into smooth dough. Cover and let stand for 20 minutes. Knead again about 1 to 2 minutes. Roll out 1/8-inch thick. Cut into strips about 1/2-inch wide and 5-inches long. Tie each strip loosely into simple knot. Drop into hot oil or shortening in mini-fryer. Fry until golden, about 1 to 1-1/2 minutes. Drain. Sprinkle with powdered sugar. Serve warm or cold. Makes about 40 ribbons.

Butterfly Cookies

Twisted dough gives a butterfly effect.

3 egg yolks, slightly beaten
1/2 teaspoon salt
1 tablespoon sugar
1/2 teaspoon rum

1/2 cup flour
Oil or shortening for frying
Sifted powdered sugar

In medium bowl, mix egg yolks, salt, sugar, rum and flour. Turn out on lightly floured board, working in a little more flour if needed to make a stiff dough. Knead until smooth, about 10 minutes. Roll out into 1 or 2 sheets about 1/16-inch thick. Cut into strips about 2-1/2" x 3". Make 3 gashes about 1-1/2-inches long nearly to the ends. Put one end through center gash and give it a twist to make butterfly appearance. Fry in hot oil or shortening in mini-fryer until light brown. Drain. Sprinkle with powdered sugar. Makes 15 to 20 cookies.

Fried Twists

A not-so-sweet snack or dessert.

2 egg yolks
1/4 cup milk
1 teaspoon grated lemon peel
1 egg white

1-3/4 cups biscuit mix
Oil or shortening for frying
Sifted powdered sugar

In medium bowl, beat egg yolks, milk and grated lemon peel. In small bowl, beat egg white until stiff, but not dry; fold into yolk mixture. Stir in biscuit mix. On lightly floured board, roll out 1/2 of dough at a time 1/16-inch thick. Cut into 5" x 2" rectangles. Make a lengthwise slit 1-inch long in center of rectangle. Slip one end of dough through the slit, forming a twist knot. Fry in hot oil or shortening in mini-fryer about 1 minute on each side, or until golden. Drain. Sprinkle with powdered sugar. Makes 24 twists.

Fried Cream

Dazzle guests with this dramatic creation.

1/4 cup sugar
1/4 teaspoon salt
3 tablespoons cornstarch
3 egg yolks, beaten
2 cups heavy cream
1 cinnamon stick

1 tablespoon dark rum
1 (2-1/4-oz.) pkg. slivered almonds
2 whole eggs, beaten
1/2 cup fine dry bread crumbs
Oil or shortening for frying
Warmed rum or brandy, if desired

In heavy saucepan, blend sugar, salt and cornstarch. Stir in 3 egg yolks and cream. Add cinnamon stick. Cook over low heat, stirring constantly, until smooth and quite thick. Remove from heat and discard cinnamon stick. Stir in 1 tablespoon rum. Spread about 1/2-inch deep in buttered 6" x 10" dish. Refrigerate several hours. Finely grind almonds in blender or grinder. Cut chilled cream mixture in 2-inch squares. Remove carefully with spatula. Dip each piece of cream mixture in almonds, then in beaten whole eggs, then in bread crumbs. Refrigerate several hours. Fry in hot oil or shortening in mini-fryer until golden, about 1 to 1-1/2 minutes. Serve plain or, if desired, arrange on heat-proof serving plate. Pour warmed rum or brandy over, and ignite with long match. Serve when flames go out. Makes 15 squares.

Pronto Date Rolls

Crescent rolls are a welcome short-cut.

1/4 cup sugar
1/4 teaspoon cinnamon

1 (8-oz.) can refrigerated crescent rolls
16 whole, pitted dates

In small bowl, combine sugar and cinnamon; set aside. Separate crescent dough into 8 triangles. Cut each in half, crosswise, forming 16 triangles. Place date on each triangle. Fold wide-angled corner over date and roll to opposite edge. Seal dough at ends of roll. Fry in hot oil or shortening in mini-fryer until deep golden brown. Drain. While warm, roll in sugar-cinnamon mixture. Makes 16 rolls.

Cottage-Cheese Puffs

Loaded with protein!

3/4 cup cottage cheese
1 egg
1/4 cup milk
1/2 teaspoon vanilla
3/4 cup flour

1-1/2 teaspoons baking powder
1/2 teaspoon salt
Oil or shortening for frying
Sifted powdered sugar, if desired
Grape or berry jelly

In medium bowl, beat cottage cheese and egg with fork or whisk until well-blended. Beat in milk and vanilla. In small bowl, mix together flour, baking powder and salt. Stir into cottage cheese mixture until blended. Drop rounded teaspoons into hot oil or shortening in mini-fryer. Fry until golden, about 2 to 3 minutes. Drain. Sprinkle with powdered sugar, if desired. Serve warm with jelly. Makes 20 to 30 puffs.

Batters & Sauces

For your convenience, each recipe in this book is complete, with the proper coating or batter and sauce if a specific one is required. In addition, I have included extra fritter batters in this section in case you want to experiment and develop recipes of your own. Use fresh fruits or vegetables from your garden and meats or fish that are special favorites with your family. Some of these are fairly standard batters, while others have a special flavor or texture, such as Beer Fritter Batter or Yeast Fritter Batter.

Beer Fritter Batter creates a very light crispy coating that's good on vegetables or fish. Yeast Fritter Batter is similar, but slightly thicker than most batters. Although it takes longer to make, it is well worth the extra time because of the different yeast flavor and the light texture. Remember to have the food dry before coating with batter.

Sauces are included with the appropriate recipes in other sections of the book. However, there are a number of sauces that are optional or a matter of personal preference. For example, some people like to squeeze lemon wedges over fish, while others prefer some type of prepared sauce. I have included several kinds of sauces that are compatible with fish and seafood. If you enjoy sauces on fried fish, you'll like the Creamy Dill Sauce or Horseradish Yogurt Sauce. For those who like a more traditional accompaniment to fried fish, use the ever-popular Tartar Sauce or Easy Seafood Sauce which is a seafood cocktail sauce.

For fresh or frozen vegetables that are coated with crumbs or encased in a batter, Sour Cream Sauce and Creole Sauce are good choices. Each is different in flavor and texture, but equally good over a variety of vegetables.

Most fruit fritters don't actually need a sauce if they are generously sprinkled with powdered sugar or served with honey or maple syrup. If you are a sauce fan, be sure to sample the Maple-Pecan Sauce or Apricot-Orange Sauce on your fritters.

Yeast Fritter Batter

A thicker batter. Try it for fish, fillets, shrimp, carrot slices, zucchini sticks, eggplant wedges and green pepper rings.

1 pkg. dry yeast
1/2 teaspoon sugar
1/4 cup warm water
1/2 teaspoon salt

1-1/2 cups flour
1 cup warm water
Oil or shortening for frying
Fish or vegetables

In small bowl, sprinkle yeast and sugar in 1/4 cup warm water. Let stand until yeast begins to foam, 8 to 10 minutes. In medium bowl, combine salt, flour, 1 cup warm water and yeast mixture. Beat with spoon until lumps disappear. Cover and let rise until doubled in bulk, about 1-1/2 to 2 hours. Stir down. Dip prepared fish or vegetables into batter. Fry in hot oil or shortening in mini-fryer until golden brown. Drain and serve warm. Makes about 3 cups batter, enough for 5 to 6 servings.

Fruit Fritter Batter

Try this wine batter with your favorite fruits.

1-1/4 cups flour
1 cup white wine
1 tablespoon sugar
1 teaspoon grated lemon peel
1/4 teaspoon salt
1 egg white

2 to 3 cups peeled, sliced raw apples,
   pears or bananas
Sifted powdered sugar
Oil or shortening for frying
Fruit sauce, if desired

In medium bowl, combine flour with wine, sugar, grated lemon peel and salt. Beat until smooth. Cover and refrigerate several hours. Just before using, beat egg white in small bowl until stiff but not dry. Fold egg white into chilled batter. Pat sliced fruit dry with paper towels. Sprinkle fruit with powdered sugar. Dip fruit into chilled fritter batter. Drop into hot oil or shortening in mini-fryer. Fry until golden brown. Sprinkle with more powdered sugar or serve with a fruit sauce, if desired. Makes enough batter for 6 servings.

Beer Fritter Batter

A light, crispy batter for vegetables or fish.

1 cup flour
1/4 teaspoon salt
1 cup flat beer

2 tablespoons cooking oil
2 egg whites
Vegetables or fish

In a medium bowl, combine flour with salt. Make a well in center; pour in beer and oil. Beat with rotary beater until smooth. Let stand for at least 1 hour. In small bowl, beat egg whites until stiff. Stir beer batter and fold in beaten egg whites. Dip prepared vegetables or fish into batter; let excess drip in bowl. Fry in hot oil or shortening in mini-fryer until golden brown. Drain and serve warm. Especially good with onions, zucchini, clams or fish. Makes about 2 cups batter, enough for 3 to 4 servings.

Quick Vegetable-Fritter Batter

Make this all-purpose batter at a moment's notice!

3/4 cup flour
1 teaspoon baking powder
1 teaspoon salt

3/4 cup milk
1 egg, slightly beaten
Vegetables

In small bowl, combine flour, baking powder and salt. Gradually add milk, then egg. Beat until smooth. Dip prepared vegetables in batter. Fry in hot oil or shortening in mini-fryer until golden brown. Drain and serve warm. Makes about 2 cups batter, enough for 3 to 4 servings.

Tempura Batter

Ice water gives this batter a lacy effect!

1 egg yolk
2 cups ice water
1/8 teaspoon baking soda

1-2/3 cups flour
Shrimp or vegetables

In medium bowl, combine egg yolk, ice water and baking soda. Stir in flour. Mix well with wooden spoon. Dip shrimp or vegetables in batter. Fry in hot oil or shortening in mini-fryer until golden. Use batter as soon as it is mixed, because the ice water helps to create the special lacy effect when coated foods are fried. Serve warm. Makes about 4 cups batter, enough for 6 servings.

Quick Chinese-Plum Sauce

Versatile with seafood or ribs.

1/2 cup chutney
1 cup plum preserves
1 tablespoon wine vinegar

1 tablespoon brown sugar
Shrimp, ribs or won ton

Chop large pieces of chutney. In small saucepan, combine chutney, plum preserves, wine vinegar and brown sugar. Heat to boiling. Serve warm over fried shrimp, ribs or won ton. Makes 1-1/2 cups sauce.

Oriental Sweet-Sour Sauce

A treat with fish or meat.

2 tablespoons cooking oil
1 clove garlic, crushed
2 carrots, thinly sliced
1 cup chicken broth or bouillon
1/2 cup sugar
1/2 cup red-wine vinegar

2 teaspoons soy sauce
2 tablespoons cornstarch
1/4 cup water
1 cup fresh Chinese pea pods,
   if desired
Fried fish, chicken or pork

In skillet, heat cooking oil and garlic. Add carrots. Stir-fry several minutes. Stir in chicken broth or bouillon, sugar, wine vinegar and soy sauce. Dissolve cornstarch in water. Add to mixture in skillet. Cook over low heat, stirring constantly, until thick and translucent. Add pea pods, if desired. Serve hot over fried fish, chicken or pork. Makes about 3 cups sauce.

Tartar Sauce

The tradition with fish!

1/2 cup mayonnaise
1/4 cup sweet-pickle relish,
  well-drained
1 teaspoon instant minced onion

1/2 teaspoon Worcestershire sauce
1 teaspoon minced parsley
Fried fish, shrimp or scallops

In small bowl, combine mayonnaise, pickle relish, onion, Worcestershire sauce and parsley. Cover and refrigerate at least 1 hour to blend flavors. Serve with fried fish, shrimp or scallops. Makes 3/4 cup sauce.

Easy Seafood Sauce

A quick sauce for seafood.

1/2 cup catsup
1 tablespoon prepared horseradish
1 teaspoon Worcestershire sauce

1 teaspoon minced instant dry onion
1 teaspoon lemon juice
Fried seafood

In small bowl, combine catsup, horseradish, Worcestershire sauce, onion and lemon juice. Refrigerate at least 1 hour to blend flavors. Serve with fried shrimp, scallops, or other fried seafoods. Makes about 1/2 cup sauce.

Cheese Relish Sauce

The ideal dip or sauce for frankfurters.

1 (10-3/4-oz.) can Cheddar cheese soup,
  undiluted
1/4 cup sweet pickle relish

1 tablespoon prepared mustard
Corn Dogs, page 72, or
  Hot Dog Puffs, page 74

In saucepan, combine soup with relish and mustard. Heat until bubbly. Serve as dip for Corn Dogs, page 72, or as sauce for Hot Dog Puffs, page 74. Makes about 1-1/2 cups sauce.

Creamy Cucumber-Dill Sauce

A great addition to any fisherman's platter.

1 small cucumber
1/2 cup dairy sour cream
1/4 cup mayonnaise
1/2 teaspoon seasoned salt

1 teaspoon finely chopped green onions
1 teaspoon dried dill weed
Fried fish or seafood

Peel cucumber, cut in half and scoop out seeds. Coarsely grate. Drain. In small bowl, combine with sour cream, mayonnaise, seasoned salt, onions and dill weed. Serve with fried fish or seafood. Makes about 1-1/4 cups sauce.

Curried Peach Sauce

A taste-tempting chicken topper.

2 tablespoons butter
1-1/2 tablespoons flour
2 tablespoons brown sugar
2 tablespoons curry powder

1/4 teaspoon salt
1 (16-oz.) can peach slices with syrup
Fried chicken

In saucepan, melt butter. Stir in flour, brown sugar, curry powder and salt. Drain peaches; reserve syrup. Pour syrup into curry mixture. Cook, stirring constantly, for several minutes until mixture thickens. Add peaches. Serve warm over fried chicken. Makes about 2 cups sauce.

Sour-Cream Sauce

A complement to veal or vegetables.

2 tablespoons flour
2 tablespoons melted butter or margarine
3/4 cup milk
1 teaspoon horseradish
1/4 teaspoon salt

1/8 teaspoon pepper
1/2 teaspoon Worcestershire sauce
1/2 cup sour cream
Veal or vegetables

In small pan, stir flour into butter or margarine. Add milk, then horseradish, salt, pepper and Worcestershire sauce. Cook, stirring constantly, over low heat until slightly thickened. Remove from heat; stir in sour cream. Serve over veal or fried vegetables. Makes about 1 cup sauce.

Horseradish Yogurt Sauce

A quick, spicy sauce that's superb with shrimp.

1 cup unflavored yogurt
2 tablespoons prepared horseradish
1/4 cup sliced green onions

1 teaspoon dry mustard
1/4 teaspoon salt
Fried fish or shrimp

In small bowl, combine yogurt, horseradish, onions, dry mustard and salt. If possible, refrigerate at least 1 hour to blend flavors. Serve with fried fish or shrimp. Makes about 1 cup sauce.

Quick Horseradish-Dill Sauce

Add zip to fried fish!

1/3 cup mayonnaise
1/4 cup minced dill pickle

1 tablespoon horseradish
Fried fish or scallops

In small bowl, combine mayonnaise with pickle and horseradish. Serve with fried fish or scallops. Makes about 2/3 cup sauce.

Creole Sauce

A bright sauce to pep up fried vegetables.

2 tablespoons butter or margarine
1/2 cup chopped onion
1/4 cup chopped green pepper
1/4 cup chopped celery
1 medium tomato, peeled and chopped

1 (8-oz.) can tomato sauce
1 (3-oz.) can sliced mushrooms, drained
1/4 teaspoon salt
1/8 teaspoon garlic salt
Fried okra, eggplant or zucchini

In saucepan, melt butter or margarine. Add onion, green pepper, celery and tomato. Cover and simmer until vegetables are tender. Stir in tomato sauce, mushrooms, salt and garlic salt. Cook another 2 to 3 minutes. Serve warm over fried okra, eggplant or zucchini. Makes about 2 cups sauce.

Apricot-Orange Sauce

Colorful sauce enhances fruit fritters.

1 cup dried apricots
1-3/4 cups water
1/4 cup sugar

1 tablespoon orange-flavored liqueur
3 to 4 drops almond extract
Banana, date or pineapple fritters

In heavy saucepan, combine apricots with water and sugar. Bring to boil; cover and simmer 1 hour. Remove from heat. Add liqueur and almond extract. Puree in food mill or blend in electric blender until smooth. Serve over banana, date or pineapple fritters. Makes about 1 cup sauce.

Special Orange Sauce

Adds flavor to fruit fritters.

1 cup orange marmalade
1/3 cup orange-flavored liqueur
2 tablespoons lemon juice

Banana or blueberry fritters, or
  fig or date won ton

In saucepan, combine marmalade, liqueur and lemon juice. Heat until marmalade melts. Serve warm over banana or blueberry fritters, or fig or date won ton. Makes about 1-1/3 cups sauce.

Maple-Pecan Sauce

Tantalizes fruit fritters!

1/4 cup butter or margarine
1/2 cup powdered sugar
2 tablespoons maple syrup

1/4 cup water
1/2 cup finely chopped pecans
Traditional Banana Fritters, page 130, if desired

In saucepan, heat butter or margarine until light brown. Cool slightly. Gradually mix in powdered sugar. Stir in syrup and water. Bring to boil; simmer 1 minute. Remove from heat. Add nuts. Serve warm. Good with Traditional Banana Fritters, page 130, or any other fruit fritters. Makes 1 cup sauce.

Hot Pots and Meat Fondues

Hot Pot, borrowed from Oriental cooking, is usually a large metal pot filled with broth or oil and surrounded by uncooked meats, fish and vegetables. Cooking is done at the table with each person cooking his own selections.

Your mini-fryer can be used the same way—on a much smaller scale. Place it in the center of the table, resting on a level heat-resistant trivet. Heat broth or oil in mini-fryer according to manufacturer's directions. Make sure you have cleaned and sliced all the vegetables and meats or fish you need. Arrange them on a platter near the mini-fryer. Then let each person pick up his own food with a fondue fork or small wire basket and cook it in the mini-fryer. Naturally, the mini-fryer can accommodate only a small portion of food as compared to a traditional Hot Pot. It is perfect for 2 to 4 servings.

The thermostatic control in a mini-fryer keeps the temperature of the broth or oil just about right for frying small pieces of flank or sirloin steak. Usually tender cuts of meat such as beef sirloin or tenderloin are used for this kind of recipe. However, marinated flank steak, sliced very thin, is a nice change. Before frying these meats, pat dry with paper towels to avoid spattering.

Meat and vegetables cooked in broth provide a flavor surprise. Small amounts should be cooked at one time to avoid overflow and to keep the broth at the right temperature. When all the meats and vegetables are cooked, unplug your mini-fryer, let cool slightly, and dip out the broth into soup mugs or bowls for each person. It's delicious!

Fondued Flank Steak

Marinade provides a hint of Oriental flavor.

1 lb. flank steak
   cut across grain 3/8-in. thick
1 cup beef bouillon
1/3 cup sherry wine

2 tablespoons soy sauce
1 clove garlic, crushed
1/8 teaspoon onion salt
Oil or shortening for frying

Place meat in shallow dish. In saucepan, heat bouillon, wine, soy sauce, garlic and onion salt. Simmer uncovered 5 minutes. Cool. Pour bouillon mixture over meat. Cover and refrigerate several hours or overnight. Drain meat. Pat dry with paper towels. Fry in hot oil or shortening in mini-fryer for 1 to 2 minutes, or until meat is desired degree of doneness. Drain. Serve hot. Makes 4 servings.

Bali Hai Steak Fondue

A taste of the tropics! You'll need skewers for this one.

1/2 cup cooking oil
1/2 cup dry red wine
2 tablespoons catsup
2 tablespoons molasses
2 tablespoons minced crystallized ginger
1/2 teaspoon salt

1 clove garlic, minced
1/2 teaspoon pepper
1/2 teaspoon curry powder
1 lb. boneless top sirloin steak
Oil or shortening for frying
Cooked, buttered rice

In small bowl, combine 1/2 cup oil, wine, catsup, molasses, crystallized ginger, salt, garlic, pepper and curry. Cut steak into very thin crosswise strips. Pour marinade over meat. Cover and let stand 2 hours. Drain well. Pat dry with paper towels. Thread meat on skewers in accordion fashion. Fry in hot oil or shortening in mini-fryer 1 to 2-1/2 minutes, or until meat is desired degree of doneness. Drain. Serve over hot buttered rice. Makes 4 servings.

Chicken-Vegetable Hot Pot

A complete meal in a pot!

1 can condensed chicken broth
1 cup water
1 boned chicken breast,
   cut up in small pieces

1 medium zucchini, sliced
2 cups fresh spinach leaves
1/4 lb. fresh mushrooms, sliced
Soy sauce

Pour chicken broth and water into unheated mini-fryer. Heat for 5 minutes. Drop in chicken pieces and zucchini. Cook 3 to 4 minutes. Add spinach and mushrooms. Cook for another 3 to 4 minutes until done. Spoon out chicken and vegetables, then broth. Serve hot with soy sauce. Makes 2 servings.

Skewered-Steak Fondue

Cook at the table in your mini-fryer.

1/2 lb. fillet of beef
   or boneless sirloin
1/2 cup soy sauce
1/4 cup dry white wine
1 tablespoon cooking oil

1 clove garlic, minced
1/2 teaspoon ground ginger
12 to 15 small fresh mushrooms
Oil or shortening for frying

Slice beef in 1/8-inch-thick strips. In medium bowl, combine soy sauce, white wine, 1 tablespoon oil, garlic and ginger. Pour over meat. Cover and refrigerate several hours or overnight. Drain meat. Pat dry with paper towels. Arrange strips of beef on 2 skewers alternately with mushrooms. Carefully drop into hot oil or shortening in mini-fryer. Fry about 1/2 to 1 minute, or until meat is desired degree of doneness. Drain and serve hot. Makes 2 servings.

Beef Hot Pot

A great idea borrowed from Oriental gourmets.

1/2 to 3/4 lb. boneless beef sirloin
  or tenderloin
4 green onions
1 or 2 summer squash, crookneck
  or zucchini

6 to 8 mushrooms
2 broccoli stalks
2 (10-1/2-oz.) cans condensed beef broth
  or bouillon
Teriyaki Sauce, see below

Teriyaki Sauce:
1/3 cup soy sauce
1 tablespoon lemon juice
1 tablespoon honey

1/4 teaspoon ground ginger
1/4 teaspoon garlic salt

Cut partially frozen beef in very thin slices. Cut green onions in 2-inch lengths. Thinly slice squash and mushrooms. Break apart broccoli flowerets into small clusters, and thinly slice stalks. Arrange meat and prepared vegetables on tray. Pour broth or bouillon into unheated mini-fryer. Bring broth or bouillon to a boil. Carefully drop in small amount of onion, squash, and broccoli; simmer about 1 minute. Add small amount of meat and a few mushrooms. Cook to desired doneness, another 1 to 2 minutes. Scoop out cooked meat and vegetables with slotted spoon or strainer. Repeat process until meat and vegetables are all cooked. Dip meat and vegetables into Teriyaki Sauce. Unplug mini-fryer. Carefully pour remaining broth into mugs or soup bowls and serve hot. Makes 2 to 3 servings.

Teriyaki Sauce:
Combine sauce ingredients; stir to blend well.

Spicy Beef Fondue

It's fun to cook this beef at the table.

1-1/2 cups chicken broth or bouillon
1/2 cup white wine
1 onion, thinly sliced
1 celery stalk, sliced
1 clove garlic, minced
6 peppercorns
1/2 teaspoon salt

1/2 teaspoon dried tarragon leaves
2 sprigs parsley
1 bay leaf
1 to 1-1/4 lbs. boneless beef sirloin
    or tenderloin cut in 1-in. cubes
Steak sauce, if desired

The day before serving, in mini-fryer combine broth or bouillon, wine, onion, celery, garlic, pepper-corns, salt, tarragon, parsley and bay leaf. Bring to a boil. Cool, pour into bowl or plastic container, cover and refrigerate overnight. Before reheating, strain mixture through a fine sieve. Pour strained broth into mini-fryer. Bring to a boil. Use fondue forks or skewers to spear cubes of meat, dip into hot broth. Cook 1/2 to 1 minute depending on desired degree of doneness. Serve plain or with steak sauce, if desired. Makes 2 to 3 servings.

Mini-Fryer Hot Pot

A mini-version of the authentic Chinese hot pot.

10 to 12 uncooked medium shrimp
1 whole chicken breast, halved, skinned
    and boned
Vegetables
3 cups chicken broth or bouillon

1 cup coarsely chopped Chinese cabbage
1/2 cup sliced celery
2 green onions, cut in 1-in. pieces
6 to 8 canned water chestnuts, sliced
Soy sauce or teriyaki sauce

Shell and devein shrimp. Cut chicken in thin slivers. Arrange shrimp and chicken on tray with prepared vegetables. Pour broth or bouillon into unheated mini-fryer. Plug in fryer; heat broth or bouillon to boiling. Carefully drop in small amounts of shrimp, chicken, Chinese cabbage and celery. Simmer about 1 minute. Add small amount of onions and water chestnuts. Cook several minutes to desired doneness. Scoop out shrimp, chicken and vegetables with slotted spoon or strainer. Repeat process until all shrimp, chicken and vegetables are cooked. Dip into soy sauce or teriyaki sauce. Unplug mini-fryer. Carefully pour remaining broth into mugs and serve hot. Makes 3 to 4 servings.

How to Make Spicy Beef Fondue

Heat vegetables, wine and herbs with chicken broth or bouillon. Cool, pour into a bowl or plastic container, cover and refrigerate overnight..

Strain broth-and-vegetable mixture just before reheating.

Let each person cook his own meat in seasoned broth in mini-fryer, using fondue forks or skewers.

Mini-Fryers With Adjustable Temperature Control

All the recipes in this book except those in this section have been designed for mini-fryers with a thermostatic control which maintains only a high temperature. That is, they reach a temperature range of 375°F to 400°F (190°C to 204°C) and then the thermostat keeps the heat within that range.

The recipes in this section are for mini-fryers with an *adjustable* temperature control. With these units, you can cook a greater variety of recipes because you can set the control for any temperature you choose, between about 180°F to 400°F (82°C to 204°C). You can turn the temperature fairly high to brown meats, then turn the control down to simmer foods.

Fryers with adjustable temperature control are especially handy for cheese dishes, because the temperature should be low. Also you can prepare a small amount of soup and then let it stay warm until serving time.

Mini-Beef Stew, scaled down to mini-fryer size, is a delicious stew for 3 or 4 people.

Cheese fondue is also possible in these fryers. You can adjust the control so it is hot enough to melt cheese, but not so hot the cheese separates. When making fondue, add small amounts of cheese at a time; stir slowly and continuously until all cheese is melted and mixture looks like a smooth thick sauce. Keep the temperature turned low while you dip in chunks of French bread. Individual fondue forks are customarily used for dipping bread into fondue but you can also use long skewers. Swirl bread cubes in fondue using a figure-8 motion. Should the fondue become too thick, add a small amount of *warmed* white wine and stir in completely.

Chicken Corn Soup

Good, hearty chicken soup with Pennsylvania influence.

3 cups chicken broth or bouillon
1 cup diced cooked chicken
1 ear corn on the cob
1/2 cup uncooked noodles

1/4 cup chopped celery
1 tablespoon chopped parsley
1/4 teaspoon salt
1/8 teaspoon pepper

In unheated mini-fryer with adjustable temperature control, combine broth or bouillon and cooked chicken. Turn control to 250°F (121°C). Cut corn off the cob. When mixture in pot boils, add corn kernels, noodles, celery, parsley, salt and pepper. Bring to a boil. Reduce heat to 220°F (104°C) and simmer 5 to 6 minutes, until noodles are tender. Makes about 5 cups of soup.

Mini Beef Stew

A traditional stew made for mini-fryers.

1 lb. beef stew meat,
   cut in 1-in. cubes
1/3 cup flour
1 tablespoon cooking oil
1 small onion, chopped
1 cup beef bouillon
1 teaspoon Worcestershire sauce
1/8 teaspoon pepper

1 teaspoon salt
1 bay leaf
1/4 teaspoon paprika
2 carrots, peeled and cut in 1-in. chunks
1 potato, peeled and cut in eighths
1/2 cup sliced celery
1 cup water

In shallow dish, coat meat with flour. Set aside excess flour. In unheated mini-fryer with adjustable temperature control, pour 1 tablespoon oil. Turn control to 350°F (177°C). Add meat and brown on all sides. Add onion, then bouillon. Turn control down to 225°F (107°C). Stir in Worcestershire sauce, pepper, salt, bay leaf and paprika. Add carrots, potatoes, celery and water. Cover and cook about 2 hours, until meat and vegetables are tender. Remove bay leaf. Thicken stew with remaining flour. Cook several minutes, stirring constantly. Makes 3 to 4 servings.

Danish-Style Cauliflower Soup

Thanks to the Danes, a different taste in soup!

2 tablespoons butter or margarine
2 green onions, chopped
2 tablespoons flour
1 cup chicken broth or bouillon
1 cup thinly sliced cauliflower

1/4 teaspoon salt
1-1/2 cups milk
1 cup grated Cheddar cheese
1 tablespoon dry white wine

In unheated mini-fryer with adjustable temperature control, place butter or margarine and onions. Turn control to 220°F (104°C). Heat until butter or margarine melts. Stir in flour. Cook 2 to 3 minutes. Add broth or bouillon, cauliflower and salt. Bring to a boil. Cover and simmer until cauliflower is tender, about 10 to 15 minutes. Stir in milk, grated cheese and wine. Heat, stirring until cheese melts. Serve hot. Makes about 3 cups soup.

Malaysian Chicken Soup

Here's an unusual, nourishing soup!

1 whole chicken breast,
   or 1 cup uncooked chicken
3 cups chicken broth or bouillon
1/2 cup chopped onion
1/8 teaspoon ground ginger

1/4 teaspoon ground coriander
1 clove garlic, minced
1/8 teaspoon cinnamon
1/2 cup cooked rice
1/2 cup fresh or canned bean sprouts

Remove bone and skin from chicken. Cut into thin strips. In unheated mini-fryer with adjustable temperature control, combine chicken with broth or bouillon. Add onion, ginger, coriander, garlic and cinnamon. Turn control to 250°F (121°C). Bring to a boil. Stir in rice. Cover and turn control to 230°F (110°C). Cook 20 minutes. Stir in bean sprouts. Heat but do not boil. Serve hot. Makes 2 to 3 servings.

Bavarian Cabbage Soup

Sausage seasons this soup just right!

1/2 lb. bulk pork sausage
1/4 cup chopped celery
1/4 cup chopped onion
1 tablespoon chopped parsley

3 cups chicken broth or bouillon
1 teaspoon Worcestershire sauce
1-1/2 cups shredded cabbage

In unheated mini-fryer with adjustable temperature control, place sausage. Turn control to 300°F (149°C). Sauté for several minutes, stirring frequently to break up pieces of meat. Spoon off excess grease. Stir in celery, onion, parsley, broth or bouillon, Worcestershire sauce and cabbage. Bring to a boil. Cover and reduce heat to about 220°F (104°C). Simmer about 5 minutes, until vegetables are tender. Serve hot. Makes about 4 cups soup.

Cheese Soup

Great with ham or turkey sandwiches.

1/4 cup butter or margarine
1 medium carrot, peeled and finely chopped
1 celery stalk, finely chopped
1 medium green onion, finely chopped
1/4 cup flour

1 cup chicken broth or bouillon
2 cups milk or light cream
1/2 teaspoon salt
1 cup grated sharp Cheddar cheese

In unheated mini-fryer with adjustable temperature control, place butter or margarine. Turn control to 250°F (121°C). Add carrot, celery and onion. Cook until onion is limp. Stir in flour and cook another 2 to 3 minutes. Add broth or bouillon, milk or light cream and salt. Bring to a boil. Turn control to slightly above 220°F (104°C). Cover and simmer about 5 minutes. Stir in grated cheese. Serve hot. Makes about 3-1/2 cups soup.

Hobo Stew

Thick and hearty; a thrifty meal-in-a-pot.

1 small onion, sliced
1/4 cup diced green pepper
2 tablespoons cooking oil
1 lb. lean ground beef
1/2 teaspoon salt
1 tablespoon bottled steak sauce

1/2 teaspoon dry mustard
1 (16-oz.) can kidney beans, drained
1 (8-oz.) can whole-kernel corn, drained
1 (16-oz.) can tomatoes
1 (8-oz.) can tomato sauce
1 small zucchini, sliced

Turn mini-fryer control to 250°F (121°C). Add onion, green pepper and oil. Cook until onion is limp. Add beef. Cook, stirring with a wooden spoon to break up large pieces of meat. Add remaining ingredients. Bring to boil. Cover, turn control slightly above 220°F (104°C), and simmer about 10 to 15 minutes. Makes 4 to 6 servings.

How To Make Hobo Stew

Cook onion, green pepper and beef before adding other vegetables.

Turn down heat to simmer stew after all ingredients have been added.

Cheesy Bean Dip

Add more hot sauce if you like spicy dips.

1 (14-oz.) can refried beans
1 (8-oz.) jar pasteurized process cheese spread
1 teaspoon chili powder

Dash red pepper sauce
Corn chips

In unheated mini-fryer with adjustable temperature control, combine beans, cheese, chili powder and pepper sauce. Turn control to 180°F (82°C). Heat until cheese melts, stirring occasionally. Serve hot, with corn chips. Makes about 2-1/2 cups dip.

Cheese Fondue

Mini-fryers make classic cheese fondue!

12 oz. grated Swiss cheese, about 3 cups
1 teaspoon cornstarch
1/2 teaspoon dry mustard
1 clove garlic, halved

3/4 cup dry white wine
1 teaspoon lemon juice
French bread, cut in cubes

In medium bowl, mix grated cheese with cornstarch and dry mustard. In unheated mini-fryer with adjustable temperature control, rub cut garlic around inside. Pour wine and lemon juice into mini-fryer. Plug in mini-fryer and turn control to 180°F (82°C). Heat until bubbles rise and cover surface. Add grated-cheese mixture by handfuls. Stir well with wooden spoon in a figure-8 motion between each handful. When cheese mixture is blended and smooth, spear bread cubes with fondue forks or skewers. Dip into fondue and swirl to coat. If fondue becomes too thick, add a little warmed wine and stir vigorously. Makes 3 to 4 servings.

Shortcut Cheese-Tuna Fondue

A quick dinner with French bread, or an appetizer with corn chips.

2 (8-oz.) jars pasteurized process
   pimiento cheese spread
1/4 cup butter or margarine
1 (7-oz.) can tuna, drained and flaked

1/4 cup chopped green pepper
1 teaspoon instant minced onion
Chunks of French bread

Turn control of adjustable temperature control mini-fryer to 180°F (82°C). Combine cheese, butter or margarine, tuna, green pepper and onion. Heat until melted, stirring occasionally. Spear bread chunks with fondue forks or skewers. Dip into fondue and swirl to coat. Makes about 2-1/2 cups.

Gringo Fondue

Tell your guests to dip in!

1/2 lb. Cheddar cheese, grated
1/2 lb. Monterey Jack cheese, grated
2 tablespoons flour
1 teaspoon chili powder
1 clove garlic, halved

3/4 cup flat beer
1 small jicama, peeled and thinly sliced
2 cups sliced cauliflower
1 large green pepper, cut in chunks

In large bowl, mix cheese, flour and chili powder with fork. In unheated mini-fryer with adjustable temperature control, rub cut garlic around inside. Leave garlic in fryer. Pour in beer. Turn control to 180°F (82°C) and heat until beer begins to bubble. Remove and discard garlic halves. Increase heat to 230°F (110°C). Add cheese mixture a handful at a time, stirring constantly, until cheese is melted and smooth. Reduce heat to 180°F (82°C). Arrange jicama and cauliflower slices and green pepper chunks on tray. Spear with fondue forks or skewers. Dip into fondue and swirl to coat. Makes about 2-1/2 cups fondue.

CONVERSION TO METRIC MEASURE

WHEN YOU KNOW	SYMBOL	MULTIPLY BY	TO FIND	SYMBOL
teaspoons	tsp	5	milliliters	ml
tablespoons	tbsp	15	milliliters	ml
fluid ounces	fl oz	30	milliliters	ml
cups	c	0.24	liters	l
pints	pt	0.47	liters	l
quarts	qt	0.95	liters	l
ounces	oz	28	grams	g
pounds	lb	0.45	kilograms	kg
Fahrenheit	°F	5/9 (after subtracting 32)	Celsius	C
inches	in	2.54	centimeters	cm
feet	ft	30.5	centimeters	cm

LIQUID MEASURE TO MILLILITERS

1/4 teaspoon	=	1.25 milliliters
1/2 teaspoon	=	2.5 milliliters
3/4 teaspoon	=	3.75 milliliters
1 teaspoon	=	5 milliliters
1-1/4 teaspoons	=	6.25 milliliters
1-1/2 teaspoons	=	7.5 milliliters
1-3/4 teaspoons	=	8.75 milliliters
2 teaspoons	=	10 milliliters
1 tablespoon	=	15 milliliters
2 tablespoons	=	30 milliliters

FAHRENHEIT TO CELSIUS

F	C
200°	93°
225°	107°
250°	121°
275°	135°
300°	149°
325°	163°
350°	177°
375°	191°
400°	205°
425°	218°
450°	232°
475°	246°
500°	260°

LIQUID MEASURE TO LITERS

1/4 cup	=	0.06 liters
1/2 cup	=	0.12 liters
3/4 cup	=	0.18 liters
1 cup	=	0.24 liters
1-1/4 cups	=	0.3 liters
1-1/2 cups	=	0.36 liters
2 cups	=	0.48 liters
2-1/2 cups	=	0.6 liters
3 cups	=	0.72 liters
3-1/2 cups	=	0.84 liters
4 cups	=	0.96 liters
4-1/2 cups	=	1.08 liters
5 cups	=	1.2 liters
5-1/2 cups	=	1.32 liters

Index

Index

Index

Index